CW00521347

# Scotland Speak

First published 2013 by Lexus Ltd
60 Brook Street, Glasgow G40 2AB
Reprinted 2016

Cover design, page design and illustrations by Elfreda Crehan
Maps drawn by András Bereznay

Contributors
Catherine Brown, food writer
Sophie Cadell
Fiona Jardine
Domhnall Uilleam Stiùbhart
Birgit Wagner
General editor: Peter Terrell

www.lexusforlanguages.co.uk

British Library Cataloguing in Publication Data
A catalogue record for this book is available from the British Library.
ISBN: 978-1-904737-24-7
Printed and bound in Europe by PULSIO SARL

LET'S say there are three Scotlands. The Scotland of cities, stunning and gaunt. The Scotland of open spaces, stunning and grand. The Scotland of the mind: inventors of television and telephone, proponents of the existence of underwater monsters, a world of jigs and reels and long traditions, a nation which was independent in heart and mind and stance long before it had its own new parliament.

This book is a guide to the distinct Scots language, urban, rural and cultural. It is aimed both at native speakers of

English and those who have learned English as a second language. It explains and exemplifies Scots vocabulary and usage and, on occasions, makes comparisons with English usage, particularly where the differences are likely to cause confusion.

These are assorted fragments of language; you're not going to find any one person in Scotland who uses all these words. The language is often remarkably localized. Scottish people from certain parts of the country or certain walks of life may well not understand some of these words (which does not decrease their Scottishness).

A few of the words listed are showing their age and are now less used in speech. These are marked OLDER SCOTS. By contrast, new words spring up. A good number of these have been labelled SLANG. And the slang is often quite regional, GLASGOW, west coast, Edinburgh, EAST COAST, Aberdonian or NORTH EAST. At the peripheries, words may spill over into northern English usage. And others (**manky**, **mingin**) which not long ago would doubtless have been perceived as only Scottish are now general English usage too. The levelling and homogenizing effects of the mass media and employment mobility, dampers on regional uniqueness, also provide carriers for catchy language to spread across borders. But, in spite of this, Scots retains its own distinct body of language.

Different spellings of Scots words are shown as well as standardized Scots spellings of English words (like **heid** or **deid**).

There are explanations of key place name elements, words which, like linguistic time capsules, remind us of the lives of the inhabitants of this country many centuries ago.

Alphabetically merged with the vocabulary are notes on key words from Scottish history and notes on cultural traditions and festivals.

You'll also find:

- an introduction to Scottish food and drink on pages 140-151

- a tiny smattering of Gaelic on pages 152-153

- some place names and whisky names that are not pronounced as you might think on page 154-157

- maps of Scotland on pages 158-160.

# Aa

**a'** all; everything

**aa** NORTH EAST all; everything

**aabody** NORTH EAST everybody

**aald** SHETLAND old

**aaricht, aaright** NORTH EAST all right

**aathing** NORTH EAST everything

**abeen** NORTH EAST OLDER SCOTS above

**aber** IN PLACE NAMES This **Brittonic** word means *mouth*. So **Aberdeen**: Donsmouth; **Lochaber**: the mouth of the loch.

**ablow** OLDER SCOTS below

**abuin, abune** OLDER SCOTS above

**ach** IN PLACE NAMES from the Gaelic *achadh* meaning *field*. So **Achnasheen**: storm field.

**adee** → NORTH EAST **fit's adee?** what's wrong?

**advocate** LEGAL SCOTS An **advocate** is a member of the Faculty of Advocates, the governing body of the Scottish legal system. They are often called on to give expert opinions. In Aberdeen, however, the word advocate just means a *lawyer*.

**advocate depute** LEGAL SCOTS a law officer appointed by the **Lord Advocate** to assist in the administration of mainly criminal matters

**ae** NORTH EAST one
**there's ae thing for sure** one thing's for sure

**aenoo** NORTH EAST just now, right now

**aff** off

**affa** NORTH EAST awfully
   **he's affa nae weel** he's not very well
   **it's affa cold in here** it's really cold in here

   Affa in Scots is not posh like the English cognate *awfully*.

**affie** afternoon
   **aw affie** all afternoon

**affy** very; awfully (but not posh in Scots)

**afore** OLDER SCOTS before

**after** → **and that was me just after ma tea** and I had just
   had my supper
   **I was just after having a wee drink** I had just had a
   drink

   **see you after** confusing to the non-Scots speaker;
   after what?, they'll think; but this just means *see you,*
   *cheerio*

**ages with** To be **ages with someone** means to be the
   same age as that person.

   **jings!, I didna realize you were ages with Uncle**
   **Jack!**

**agley** OLDER SCOTS awry, wrong; crooked
   **the best laid plans of mice and men gang aft agley** a
   much-quoted line from Robert Burns. Often just the first
   part is said: **ach well, the best laid plans...**

**ah** rendering of the first person pronoun *I*

**ahin(t)** NORTH EAST behind

**aiblins** OLDER SCOTS perhaps

**ain** own

**aince** OLDER SCOTS once

**aipple** apple

**airchie** NORTH EAST posh, high-class

**airt** 1) OLDER SCOTS direction; region 2) art
**back tae his hame airt** back to his own part of the world
**in rural airts** in rural areas

**Alba** [pronounced AL-UH-PUH] the Gaelic name for Scotland

**ald** NORTH EAST old

**ale** NORTH EAST In the North East **ale** is any fizzy drink (like **ginger** in Glasgow). It isn't beer.

**alow** NORTH EAST below

**amna** OLDER SCOTS am not; aren't (when used with *I*)

**anaith** NORTH EAST beneath

**anent** OLDER SCOTS about, concerning

**aneth** NORTH EAST under

**angina-on-a-plate** a humorous name for a Scottish invention, the deep-fried Mars® Bar, which you can buy at (some) fish and chip shops

**Antonine Wall** This is the 37 mile (59.5km) long Roman wall which spanned Scotland at its narrowest point from the Firth of Forth to the Firth of Clyde. It was constructed around 139 AD on the orders of the Roman Emperor Antoninus Pius. The wall was built of turf with a broad ditch to the north. Its purpose was to defend the northern boundary of the Roman Empire. But it was only occupied for a short time. Several forts and signal towers have been uncovered and the most visible remains of the wall can be seen near Falkirk.

**ard** IN PLACE NAMES from the Gaelic *àird* meaning
*promontory* or *point*. So **Ardbeg**: little headland;
**Ardmore**: big point.

**Armadillo** Glaswegians like making up cute names for
buildings in their city. This one is a concert hall, the Clyde
Auditorium.

**aroon** around

**Arthur's Seat** The big hill rising in the centre of
Edinburgh, an extinct volcano close to the Scottish
parliament.

**ashet** NORTH EAST large, oval serving plate

**ask for** → **Fiona was asking for you** Fiona was asking
*after* you, was asking how you were; it's not that Fiona
wanted you.

**at** that

> In spoken Glaswegian Scots the *th* often disappears.
>   **ats nae right** that's not right
>   **izzat right?**
>   **at beats everything**

**athoot** NORTH EAST without

> ye canna gin oot athoot a jaikit

**athort** OLDER SCOTS across

**auch** IN PLACE NAMES from the Gaelic **achadh** meaning *field.* So **Auchenshuggle**: field of rye.

**auchter** IN PLACE NAMES from the Gaelic **uachdar** meaning *high land* or *upper part.* So **Auchermuchty**: upland area where pigs are kept.

**aul, auld** old

> **Auld Alliance** This is the name given to the long-standing friendship between Scotland and France (traditionally in a joint stand against England). In the past it was documented in treaties lending support in various ways (the original treaties being dated October 1295) with links being forged both politically and through marriage. Nowadays it has lost its political importance and is used in a more general sense.

*Glasgow's Armadillo to the left of the new Hydro and the old Finnieston crane*

**auld lang syne** long long ago

The song by Robert Burns is one of Scotland's gifts to the world and has become an international standard. The whole poem is hardly ever sung in its entirety. The following two verses and chorus will stand you in good stead.

> Should auld acquaintance be forgot,
>   And never brought to mind?
> Should auld acquaintance be forgot,
>   And auld lang syne?

*Chorus*

> For auld lang syne, my dear,
>   For auld lang syne,
> We'll tak a cup o' kindness yet,
>   For auld lang syne.

*last verse*

> And there's a hand, my trusty fiere!
>   And gies a hand o' thine!
> And we'll tak a right gude-willie waught,
>   For auld lang syne

*Chorus*

> For auld lang syne etc.

> *fiere = friend*
> *tak a right gude-willie waught = take a good old*
>   *swig or two*

**auld-farrant** OLDER SCOTS old-fashioned, old-style

**Auld Reekie** Edinburgh, the old smoky place

**ava** NORTH EAST at all
   **nae use ava** no use at all

**aw** all

**awa** away
   **come awa, quinie** come on, girl

---

In the North East **awa** can also mean *dead*.

---

**away**

---

A basic word in the Scots vocabulary, with a wide
range of uses, such as:
   **away oot and get some milk from the Spar** will you
   go out and get some milk from the Spar
   **away! not three thousand!** *expresses surprise and
   disbelief*
   **away raffle yerself!** don't be silly!
   **come away in** come on in
   **that you away hame?** are you going home?

Confusion can arise from one particular use.
   **is Dougie in there with you? – no, he's away**

The answer means:
   no, Dougie has just left
but is puzzling to non-Scots speakers, who are more
likely to understand the answer as meaning:
      no, Dougie is absent
or:  no, Dougie's on holiday
or:  no, Dougie's travelling on business
and who might even reply with:

   no, he's not away, I saw him down the corridor just
   ten minutes ago

so causing at best bewilderment, at worst an
argument.

---

**ay** IN PLACE NAMES a common ending, from the Norse *ey* or *øy* meaning island. So **Pabbay**: priest's island.

**aye**

> Three main meanings to this core Scots word:
>
> 1) yes
>
> 2) hello
>    **aye aye** hello
>
> 3) OLDER SCOTS always; still
>    **he wis aye there, sitting by the fire**
>
> **Aye** can also be used as a tag word at the end of a question to show that the person asking the question expects the answer to be *yes*.
> **you'll bring them back the morra aye?** you'll bring them back tomorrow, won't you?
>
> And there's also:
>    **aye night** one night
>
> and
>
> **Yours aye** a slightly old-fashioned but common conclusion to a letter: yours ever

**ayont** OLDER SCOTS beyond

**ayre** SHETLAND beach

# Bb

**babby** baby, a sentimentalized word

**bachle** little man, insignificant little man (not to be confused with **bauchle**)

**back** → **at the back of seven** just after seven o'clock, maybe five or ten minutes past. Interestingly, there is no corresponding expression for the time just before the hour.

**back close** the back part of the common entrance to a traditional tenement

*daylight filters through into the back close*

**baffies** slippers

**bag off** SLANG get off with someone
**by the end of the party everybody had bagged off, except me** by the end of the party everybody had got themselves a partner, except me

**baggie** 1) minnow 2) NORTH EAST (little) bag

**bahookie** SLANG backside, butt

**bairen** NORTH EAST child, baby

**bairn** child

> This can also be used as a verb.
> **he bairned her** he made her pregnant

**baith** both

**bal** IN PLACE NAMES from the Gaelic **baile** meaning *village*. So **Ballachulish**: village on the narrows.

**balloch** IN PLACE NAMES from the Gaelic **bealach** meaning *pass.*

**ballop** flies (*on trousers*)

**Balmoral Castle** The royal castle between Braemar and Ballater in Deeside, still the summer holiday residence of the Queen and royal family, was a favourite resort of Queen Victoria and Prince Albert, who oversaw building work in 1855.

**bam** SLANG short for **bampot**, crazy person
**put that doon, ye bam!** put that down, you idiot!

**bammy** SLANG crazy

**bampot** SLANG lunatic

**banjo** SLANG This can be used as a verb, meaning *to hit*.

the wee lassie banjoed him wi her handbag

**bank notes** Scottish banks still issue their own notes (there are three types: Clydesdale, Bank of Scotland and Royal Bank of Scotland). The one-pound note, now extinct in England, still lives on in Scotland, though these days a rare sight. Internationally, Scottish bank notes still have some way to go to achieve full recognition and travellers from Scotland may have problems changing Scottish notes abroad.

**banks-broo** SHETLAND cliff edge

**Bannockburn (Battle of)** In this battle, which took place in June 1314, Robert I of Scotland (Robert the Bruce) defeated Edward II of England. It proved to be decisive in the Scottish Wars of Independence and eventually led to the signing of the Treaty of Edinburgh, which recognized Scotland's independence. A visitor centre now marks the battle site near Stirling.

**bap** NORTH EAST a soft roll

**bar** IN PLACE NAMES from the Gaelic **bàrr** meaning *top* or *height*. So **Dunbar**: fort of the height.

**Barras** (Barrows) a Glasgow market, a source of cheap CDs, DVDs, clothes and some antiques

**barry** EAST COAST SLANG great, brilliant, fantastic, beautiful

**Bass Rock** A volcanic plug rising to over 100 metres out of the Firth of Forth. Home to the hermit St Baldred in the 9th century, it became a state prison in the 17th, was occupied for three years from 1691 by **Jacobites**, and is now of world importance to ornithologists as home to a major colony of gannets and other seabirds.

**bauchle** old, worn-out shoe

**baw** 1) ball 2) cry

> that kid is bawin its eyes oot

**bawbag** SLANG 1) scrotum 2) someone stupid or useless. The hurricane that hit Scotland in 2011 was nicknamed Hurricane Bawbag, presumably just because it annoyed a lot of people.

**baw-faced** SLANG with a round, chubby face. In context this is often used like **bawheid** to imply that the person with the round face is a bit of an idiot.

**bawheid** SLANG This is literally a person with a big round face which the Scots find amusing and worthy of a special term. It's normally used as a fairly cheeky form of address.
**whit ye dae that fur, ye great glaikit bawheid!** what'd you do that for, you stupid great fathead!

**beamer** → **to get a beamer** to go red in the face

**beauty** → **ya beauty!** great! brilliant!

**bed recess** an alcove, usually in the kitchen of a traditional tenement flat, which was formerly used as a sleeping area; often repurposed these DIY days as a cosy dining space

**been** NORTH EAST also: bone

**beet** NORTH EAST boot

**beg** IN PLACE NAMES from the Gaelic *beag* meaning little. So **Inverbeg**: little river mouth.

**ben**[1] IN PLACE NAMES from the Gaelic *beinn* meaning *mountain* or *hill.* So **Ben Wyvis**: huge mountain; **Benbecula**: hill of the fords.

## ben²

> A preposition meaning *in* or *into* but which is not quite so easy to tie down to a single English equivalent.
> **come ben the house** come on in
> **away ben and fetch ma...** go into the next room and fetch my...
> **come on ben the sitting room** come into the sitting room
> **he went ben the back of the hoose** he went through to the back of the house
> **she went ben the house** This doesn't mean that she went into the house, but that she went into another room.

**bendy juice** SLANG alcohol

**ben end** the inner room of a **but and ben** cottage

**Ben Nevis** At 4406 feet or 1344 metres, this is Scotland's and Britain's highest mountain (but not the most spectacular).

**bere** NORTH EAST [pronounced BARE] barley

**berkie** → SLANG **to throw a berkie** to go beserk; to have a fit

**berren** NORTH EAST child; children; otherwise written as **bairn(s)**

**Bertie Auld** RHYMING SLANG cold

> The 1960s Celtic football star has entered the world of rhyming slang.
> **bit Bertie Auld in this room, eh?**

**besom** an annoying or unpleasant woman

**bevvied up** drunk

**bevvy** drink
 **fancy a wee bevvy?** fancy a drink?
 **they've been oot on the bevvy** they've been out drinking

**bevvy-merchant** drinker

**Bhoys** Celtic football players

**bide** NORTH EAST 1) stay 2) live

> This is old or very literary in southern English but still in everyday use in North East Scotland.
> **you go then, I'm biding here** you go then, I'm staying here
> **is this far Hector bides?** is this where Hector lives?

**bidie-in** an unmarried partner (particularly female) living in the same house

**big yin** big one; big person

> A friendly way of addressing someone who the speaker sees as being taller (or more important) than himself. Billy Connolly is known in Glasgow as the Big Yin.

**bigg** SHETLAND build

**biggin** building; house

**bile** boil

**Billy(-boy)** SLANG derogatory for Protestant

**birk** NORTH EAST birch tree. The word is nowadays known to most Scots through association with the Burns song 'The Birks o' Aberfeldy'.

**birl** whirl, swing

> **if a lassie goes to a ceilidh she must expect to be birled about**

**bit** This can also mean *place, house.*

> **we all went back tae his bit for a bevvy**

**bittick** NORTH EAST OLDER SCOTS a little bit

**bittie** → NORTH EAST **a bittie** a bit, a little

**black house** Made of turf, with a roof of thatch or moss, no chimney, an open peat fire inside, they were found mainly in the Western Highlands.

**black-affronted** absolutely mortified
   **I was black-affronted** I could've died with
   embarrassment

**blaeberry** bilberry

**blair** IN PLACE NAMES from the Gaelic *blàr* meaning *plain* or
   *open land*. So **Blairgowrie**: goat plain.

**blate** NORTH EAST OLDER SCOTS shy

**blaw** blow

**bleed** NORTH EAST also the noun: blood

**bleezin** NORTH EAST SLANG drunk, smashed, plastered

**bleish of rain** NORTH EAST downpour

**blended** A blended is a whisky made from the output
   of more than one distillery, as contrasted with a **single
   malt**.

*a black house*

**blether** This can be a verb and a noun.
  **she's a right wee blether** she's a proper little chatterbox
  **we had a good blether** we had a good old chat
  **what's that damn woman blethering on about now?**

**blin** blind

**blin drift** NORTH EAST drifting snow; heavy snowfall; driving blizzard

**blyde** SHETLAND glad

**blythe** OLDER SCOTS contented; a variant of **blyde**, but only really encountered in literary works

**boaby** SLANG willie, penis

**boak** vomit
  **it gies me the boak** it makes me sick
  **he gies me the dry boak** he makes me absolutely sick

**bodie** → **a bodie** you, people

  **a bodie needs someone to talk to**

**boggin** SLANG stinking; disgusting

**bogy** → **the game's a bogy** the game's up, it's all over, you might as well forget it, it'll never work

**boil** → SLANG **away boil yer heid** go away; don't give me that nonsense; don't be stupid

**boiling** a boiled sweet

**boke** same as **boak**

**bonnet** any hat, especially a flat hat

**bonnie** pretty, beautiful
  **bonnie sair** pretty sore

**bonspiel** curling match

**bonxie** SHETLAND great skua

**bosie** NORTH EAST 1) cuddle 2) bosom
**och, come to mammy for a bosie** let mummy cuddle it better

**bothie** This is a mountain or forest hut where walkers can stop for the night (just walk in and leave it as you found it, or better). No booking, no keys. Bothies are basic, one up from a tent. You might find a wood-burning stove, but don't expect furniture or cutlery. And in place of a loo, you'll find a shovel. The word *bothie* can also be used for a hut on a building site or a rest room, say, for bus drivers.

**bottlin** Just before a girl is going to get married, her friends might get her dressed up and take her through the streets or around the offices or around the shop floor, inviting passing men to have a kiss from the bride-to-be in exchange for a small sum of money (useful for wedding presents). This is a pretty raucous custom, involving a lot of singing and tin-banging and tambourine-shaking, a bit alarming for those who don't know what's going on, and, not really surprisingly, it's on the way out in the modern world.

**bowf** bark

**bowfin** disgusting

**bowly** SLANG [bow pronounced to rhyme with COW] bowlegged

**boy**

> Can mean a man of any age. It is often used to refer to a labourer; so a stonemason might say:
> **I could'nae get the boys tae come oot oan a public holiday**

**bra** OLDER SCOTS good; brave

**brack** NORTH EAST dark fruit loaf

**brae** hill

> The word is originally Gaelic, **bràigh** meaning *hillside* or *slope*. So **Braemar**: the upper part of Mar.

**Braemar Gathering** Annual **highland games** held in September and traditionally attended by members of the royal family.

**bramble**, **brammle** NORTH EAST blackberry

**brar** brother

**braw** good; great

**bread** IN PLACE NAMES from the Gaelic **braghaid** meaning *heights*. So **Breadalbane**: the upper part of Alba (Alba being the Gaelic for Scotland).

**bree** 1) liquid 2) broth 3) GLASGOW brother

**breeks** trousers; pants

**breeng** → **smoke came breenging in** the smoke came rushing in

**breether** NORTH EAST brother

**brick** → **in wi the bricks** If you are **in wi the bricks**, you are a long-serving employee, part of the furniture.

> old Jamie thought he wis in wi the bricks, till he had a chat wi the boss last week

**brig** bridge

**brikks** trousers; pants

**Brittonic** one of the old Celtic languages

**broch** Brochs are prehistoric (2nd and 3rd century BC) round, tower-like structures, built with dry stone walls which are hollow nearer the top. They are found only in Scotland.

**broo** dole, unemployment benefit

**brosey** NORTH EAST big, burly, strapping

**bruaich** IN PLACE NAMES from the Gaelic **bruthach** meaning *hill*. So **Tighnabruaich**: house on the hill.

**bruck** SHETLAND rubbish

**bubbliejock** OLDER SCOTS a turkey

**buckie** 1) whelk 2) **Buckie**, short for Buckfast®, fortified wine produced by English monks and a big favourite of Scots **neds**, **schemies**, **jakeys** and others.

**bunker** a kitchen cabinet

**bunnet** variant of bonnet, hat

**burden** LEGAL SCOTS A burden is a restriction on the use of land or property.

**burn** stream

**Burns Night** The birthday of Scotland's national poet is celebrated across the country on 25 January every year. This traditionally takes the form of a Burns Supper where **haggis**, **neeps** and **tatties** are eaten. There may also be poetry readings, singing and a **ceilidh**.

**burroo** dole
**on the burroo** on the dole, receiving unemployment benefit

**but**

In Scots this can be positioned at the end of a sentence to act as an emphasizer.
→

> **that's really great but!** that's just really great!
> **this is no place to be in winter but!** this is definitely
> no place to be in winter!
> **you found me quick but!** you found me pretty
> quick, didn't you!

**but and ben** a home consisting of just a kitchen and a
living room, usually a cottage

**but end** NORTH EAST the outer room or kitchen of a **but and
ben** cottage

**buttery** a croissant-like roll from the North East

**button up** → **d'ye think ma heid buttons up the back?**
do you think I'm stupid?

**bygaun** → NORTH EAST OLDER SCOTS **in the bygaun** by the
way

**byke** wasps' nest

**byoch** NORTH EAST belch

*a but and ben*

# Cc

**caa** NORTH EAST call

**caald** SHETLAND cold

**caddy lamb** SHETLAND pet lamb

**cairn** IN PLACE NAMES from the Gaelic *càrn* meaning a *rocky hill* (as well as the sense of a pile of stones marking a summit). So **Cairngorm**: blue hill.

**cal** NORTH EAST cold

**caller** NORTH EAST fresh

**came** → **she has came** Use of the preterite instead of the past participle is common in speech, especially in Glaswegian dialect.

**can**

> In some regions (mainly the north) you'll still hear variant uses.
> **I'll can dae it the morn** I'll be able to do it tomorrow
> **I might can help ye** I might be able to help you

**canna, cannae** can't

**canny** sly, astute; (*with money*) careful

**cantation** NORTH EAST OLDER SCOTS discussion; dialogue

**cappie** NORTH EAST an ice-cream cone

**carnaptious** bad-tempered, irrascible

**carry-out** take-away; a meal or some drinks to take away; a place that sells food to take away

> we could get a carry-out and go back to my place
> there used to be a Chinese carry-out round here

**carse** the land beside a river

*a ceilidh*

**cartoon** NORTH EAST In the North East a **cartoon** can be used to mean a *carton,* as in a carton of milk.

**case** → **he's been gettin on my case** he's been getting on my nerves, annoying me

**catched** NORTH EAST caught

**cauld** cold

**caunle** candle

**caur** tram; car

**ceilidh** [pronounced KAY-LEE] There'll be a band playing traditional Scottish music with fiddle and accordion and drums (or possibly some or all of these replaced by a

Yamaha®), Scottish dancing, tables and chairs set out around the room. And drink and food. (Traditionally, a ceilidh was a night spent telling stories and singing songs around a peat fire in Gaelic-speaking communities.)

**Celtic Connections** [pronounced KELTIC, not SELTIC (which is the football team)] Annual festival held in Glasgow early in the year which celebrates Celtic and traditional music from Scotland and around the world (includes concerts, workshops, masterclasses and competitions).

**ceud mìle fàilte** [pronounced KEE-UT MEEL-IH FAALTCHUH] Gaelic for one hundred thousand welcomes

**chaave** struggle

**chaavin awa** NORTH EAST OK, not bad. This is a typical response to the question **fit like?**

**chaff** chat

**chaffin awa** NORTH EAST working away, working hard; see also **chaavin awa**

**champit** mashed

**chap** knock
   **chap the door** knock at the door
   **if I'm in Partick the morrow I'll come by and chap your door** I'll come round to visit

**chappit** mashed

**chaumer** NORTH EAST room

**cheeper** kiss, peck

**chib** 1) stab; slash 2) knife; weapon

**chieftain** → **great chieftain o' the puddin race** a haggis, as glorified in Burns' poem 'Address to a Haggis'.

**chiel** guy, fellow

**chipper** NORTH EAST fish and chip shop; in other parts of Scotland it is known as a **chippie.** The word can also mean *fish and chips.*

> **we picked up a chipper on the way back from the pub**

**chippie** a fish and chip shop

**chitter** NORTH EAST shiver

**chittery bite** NORTH EAST a small snack eaten after swimming to stop you from shivering

**chookie** SLANG idiot

**chookie bird** tweetie-pie, little bird (as used by an adult talking to a little child)

**chorie** SLANG thieve
   **to be on the chorie** to be thieving, to be a thief

**choryin spree** SLANG thieving expedition

**chowie** chew

**chowk** NORTH EAST cheek

**chuckies** NORTH EAST pebbles

**chuddie** chewing gum

**chuffing awa** NORTH EAST same as **chaavin awa**

**chum**

> In Scots this can also be used to form a verb.
> **I'll chum you intae town** I'll go into town with you to keep you company
> **he chummed her back to the station**

**clachan** IN PLACE NAMES a Gaelic word meaning *village*

**claethes** clothes

**claik** OLDER SCOTS talk

**clamjamfry** mess, odds and ends, clutter

**Clan system** The word *clan* comes from the Gaelic
**clann** meaning *family* or *children* and most members of
a clan will share a common descent. However, not all
people with the same surname necessarily belong to the
same (or any) clan. Clans were more established in the
Highlands and islands than in the Lowlands and were
headed by the chief who also acted as judge in legal
disputes and would call upon his men to follow him into
battle when the need arose. The land the clan lived on
was owned by the chief and the main wealth derived from
it came from cattle. In the 18th century and particularly as
a result of measures imposed after the battle of **Culloden**,
the power wielded by the clans diminished.

**clap** pat; stroke

**clappie** NORTH EAST pat; stroke

**gie the horsie a wee clappie, he'll no hurt ye** give the
horse a little pat, he
won't hurt you

**clarsach** a traditional
Celtic harp, smaller
than a classical harp
with levers rather than
pedals used to change
key. It has experienced
a revival in recent years
with events such as
the annual Edinburgh
International Harp
Festival helping to
promote interest in the
instrument.

**clartit** NORTH EAST caked, covered (in mud, make-up etc)

**clarty, clatty** dirty

> **Clearances** In the late 18th and early 19th century landowners in the Highlands and islands discovered that they could make more money from rearing sheep on their land than they could from the tenants who had been working the same land for generations. The tenants were (often forcibly) evicted from their homes. Poverty, combined with the famine of 1846, led many to emigrate to Australia and North America.

**cleg** horsefly

**close**

> common entrance and stairwell of a tenement block; everybody who lives off that staircase
> **the whole close could hear him coming home**
> **yer up the wrang close there** you're barking up the wrong tree there

**cludgie** SLANG loo; toilet

**Clyde** → **I've no just come up the Clyde in a banana boat** I'm not stupid, not naive

**clype** tell tales
**you wee clype, you!** you telltale!

**coin** NORTH EAST a less common spelling of **quine**

**come over** → NORTH EAST **there's nothing coming over me** there's nothing wrong with me

> **Common Ridings** These events take place in various towns in the Borders over the summer. Groups of horsemen ride around the boundaries of the town. The ceremonies date back to the time when the Border regions were disputed land and had to be defended.

**continue** LEGAL SCOTS If a court case is **continued**, this means that it is postponed until a later date.

**coo** cow

**cookie-mouthed** EAST COAST fond of eating biscuits and buns

**coorie in** snuggle up, cuddle up

**coorse** NORTH EAST 1) coarse 2) difficult

**Corbett** any Scottish mountain over 2,500 feet (762m) and under 3,000 feet (915m)

**corrie-fisted** left-handed

**coup¹** [pronounced COWP] 1) rubbish tip 2) mess
**see his room, some coup eh?** his room's a right mess

**coup²** 1) knock over 2) fall over

so he stands up and coups his biryani all ower her

**coupon** SLANG 1) face 2) head

ah've got a sair coupon

**Court of Session** LEGAL SCOTS the Scottish supreme civil court, sitting in Edinburgh

**couthie** OLDER SCOTS 1) friendly 2) cosy and comfortable, but often tending these days to mean twee and traditional as opposed to modern and cool

**cowk** NORTH EAST retch

**cowking** → NORTH EAST SLANG **I was cowking when Aberdeen lost** I was sick when Aberdeen lost

**cowp** same as **coup**

**craa** SHETLAND hooded crow

**crabbit** bad-tempered; morose; surly

**crack** chat; good conversation

> **all five of us spent the night in the pub, it was good crack**
>
> Also a verb:
>
> **ah cracked wi the barman a while aboot...**
>
> In the North East this is also used to mean *to strike* as in **to crack a spunk** (strike a match).

**craic** another spelling of **crack**, the noun

**craig** OLDER SCOTS neck

**crannie** NORTH EAST little finger

**crannog** an ancient loch-dwelling, used as far back as mesolithic times. Some crannogs are still used by Scots as places to fish from or to moor alongside.

*a craw-stepped gable*

**craw** → **shoot the craw** SLANG leave, go away, scarper, do a runner

**craw-stepped gable** a traditional Scots architectural feature

**cream puff** → RHYMING SLANG **take the cream puff** go into a huff, get offended

**creamer** NORTH EAST 1) an ice-cream shop 2) an ice-cream van

**creelin** same as a **bottlin**

**croft** small farm, small holding

**Crown Office** LEGAL SCOTS the Scottish office responsible for the prosecution of crime

**crunk her up!** NORTH EAST SLANG get a move on!, hurry up!

> **crunk her up, ah've nae got a' day!**

**cry** also means *to call*
**cry it what ye like** call it what you like
**what d'ye cry that instrument he's playing?**

**cuddie** horse

**Cuillins** mountains on Skye

> **Culloden** This battle took place in 1746 between the **Jacobites** under Bonnie Prince Charlie and the Hanoverians under the Duke of Cumberland. The terrain – open moorland near Inverness – was unsuited to the Jacobites' style of fighting and they suffered a huge defeat in what was the last pitched battle on British soil.

**curn** → **a curn...** a few...

**cutty sark** OLDER SCOTS a short, woman's shirt

# Dd

**da**[1] dad

**da**[2] SHETLAND the

**da**[3] NORTH EAST don't
    **da ken** dunno
    **da hae time** don't have time
    **I da agree** I don't agree

**dae** do

**dal** IN PLACE NAMES from the Gaelic *dail* meaning *field* or *dale*.
    So **Dalkeith**: field of the wood, wood field.

**dan** SHETLAND then

**Dan** SLANG derogatory for Catholic

**darg** work; day's work

**dat** SHETLAND that

**daunder, dauner** stroll

**de** SHETLAND you

> In Shetland the word **du** for *you* has different case
> endings, like a Germanic or Scandinavian language.
>   **dat is fir de** that's for you

**dear green place** Glasgow

**Declaration of Arbroath** A Latin document
written in 1320 asserting Scotland's claim for
independence from England and its right to freedom.
Bearing the seals of Scottish earls and barons, it was
sent to Pope John XXII. The Declaration of Arbroath
served as a model for the American Declaration of
Independence.

**dee** 1) die 2) NORTH EAST do

**Dee** → NORTH EAST **ah've nae just come doon the Dee on a digestive** I'm not stupid, wasn't born yesterday. This is a parallel to the Glaswegian expression about the **Clyde** and banana boats.

**deek** EAST COAST SLANG look at; look; see
**deek that wee gadgie in the kilt** look at that little guy in the kilt
**ah cannae deek ony change** I can't see any change
Also a noun.
**take a deek at this video** take a look at this video

**deem** NORTH EAST girl

**deep-fried Mars® Bar** a Scottish invention, affectionately known as **angina-on-a-plate**

**deid** [pronounced DEED] dead

**deif** [pronounced DEEF] deaf

**depute** In administrative language a **depute** is the equivalent of a *deputy*.

> **the Depute Director of Parks**

**Desperate Dan** As well as being the name of a well-known cartoon character, this is also used to refer to a large-format steak and kidney pie.

**deuk** SHETLAND a duck

**dicht** wipe; clean

**didgy** SLANG dustbin

**didna, didnae** didn't

**ding doon** pelt down

> **with the rain dingin doon**

**dinger** → SLANG **to go yer dinger**
1) to be very energetic 2) to be very angry; also used with the verb *do* or **dae** or **dee**

**he's deen his dinger the day** he's really going for it today

**wi the wee dug's tail daein its dinger at ye like that ye have to give in** when the little dog's tail wags away at you like that, you have to give in

**dingy** SLANG [pronounced to rhyme with CLINGY] ignore

**ah did ask but ye jist dingied me**

**dinna, dinnae** don't

**dippet** SLANG daft, stupid

**direction** OLDER SCOTS This can also mean *address* in North Eastern usage.

**dirk** the traditional Highlander's dagger

**dirl** NORTH EAST noise

**keep yer dirl doon!**

**dirler** 1) In the Glasgow area a **dirler** is a person who sings mouth music.
2) In the North East a **dirler** is a toilet.

**disna, disnae** doesn't

**dispone** LEGAL SCOTS To **dispone** land or property is to transfer ownership of it.

**div** NORTH EAST do
**I div like...** I do like...

**dizna, diznae** doesn't

**dizzen** OLDER SCOTS dozen

**dochter** OLDER SCOTS daughter

**dock** NORTH EAST SLANG bottom, bum

**dod** piece, dollop

> **a big dod of cream**

**doh** → **up to high doh** very worried; nervous; in a state of great excitement

**dominie** NORTH EAST OLDER SCOTS schoolmaster

**Donald** any Scottish mountain south of the **Highland line** that is higher than 2,000 feet (610m)

**Donald** RHYMING SLANG short for **Donald Duck**, which means *luck*

**Dons** → **the Dons** nickname for Aberdeen Football Club

**doo** dove

**dook** soak
**to go for a dook** to go for a swim
**to dook for apples** to try to get apples out of a bucket of water using your teeth – an old Halloween game

**dookers** swimming trunks

**dooket** 1) dovecote 2) pigeonhole

**doolie** fool

**doon** down

**doot** same as **doubt**

**Doric** Doric is the distinctive Scots language of north-east Scotland, particularly of Aberdeen and its surrounding region.

**doss** SLANG stupid

**dottled** NORTH EAST confused

## doubt

> In Scots this also means *to expect* or *to think* – the exact opposite of *doubt*. (French has a similar construction in *se douter* = to suspect).
>
> **I doubt ye've got a wrang number** I think you've got the wrong number
>
> **I doubt ye're richt** I expect you're right

**douce** gentle; refined

**dour** IN PLACE NAMES from the old Gaelic **dobhar** meaning *water*. So **Aberdour**: mouth of the river Dour.

**dout¹** cigarette end

**dout²** NORTH EAST go to **doubt**

**downie** continental quilt

**dowp** NORTH EAST backside, bottom

**dram** a drink of whisky, no longer a specific measure though

**drap** drop

**dreich** [pronounced DREECH with the CH as in loch] grey and dismal

> **one more dreich weekend like this and that's me aff tae Barcelona**

**drookit, droukit** soaked, drenched

**drouth** NORTH EAST 1) drinker 2) thirst 3) dryness

**drouthy** thirsty

**drum** IN PLACE NAMES from the Gaelic **druim** meaning *ridge*. So **Drummore**: big ridge; **Drumnadrochit**: ridge bridge.

**drumlie** murky (*water, liquid*)

**dry stane dyke** dry-stone wall

*fancy a wee dram before the hearse gets here, Archie?*

**du** SHETLAND in Shetland the English word *you*

> Shetland retains the distinctions of different words for
> *you*, that exist in other European languages, but which
> have long since disappeared in English. In Shetland the
> word *you* is either reserved for people seen as social
> superiors or it is just the plural form of **du**.

**dubbie** muddy

**dubs** mud; puddles

**dug** dog

**dum, dun** IN PLACE NAMES from the Gaelic **dùn** meaning
   *fortress* or *mound*. So **Dumbarton**: fortress of the Britons;
   **Dunblane**: St Blane's hill; **Dunkeld**: fort of the Caledonians.

**dumfounert** dumbfounded, stunned

**dun** IN PLACE NAMES same as **dum**

**dunnie** 1) cellar 2) the passageway of the **back close**, which is low down and dark

**dunt** a heavy blow
   **he got the dunt** NORTH EAST he got the sack

**dunter** SHETLAND eider duck

**Dux** At school the **Dux** is the pupil with the highest overall marks in the top year. He/she receives an award for this.

**dwaam, dwam** → **to be away in a dwaam** to be in a dream, to be in a daze

**dy** SHETLAND your
   **tak du dy time** you take your time

**dyke** a wall, as around a field

*away in a dwaam while the others work*

# Ee

**eccle** IN PLACE NAMES from the Gaelic *eaglais* meaning *church*. So **Ecclefechan**: church of St Beachan.

**edin** IN PLACE NAMES from the Gaelic *aodann* meaning *slope*. So (possibly) **Edinburgh**: fortress on the hill.

**Edinburgh** Scotland's capital city and location of many of the country's most important historical, political and cultural institutions, including the new Scottish parliament. Edinburgh plays host to a fair **wheen** of festivals, including the **Edinburgh International Book Festival**, in August every year, the **Edinburgh International Jazz and Blues Festival**, July/August, the **Edinburgh Festival** the famous annual arts festival showcasing some of the top orchestras and theatre companies from around the world, end August-September and the **Edinburgh Military Tattoo** which runs for several weeks over the summer with marching bands, bagpipes, dancing and fireworks.

**ee** OLDER SCOTS eye; note the unusual plural form: **een**

**eedjit** idiot

**eela** SHETLAND sea-angling

**een** 1) one 2) OLDER SCOTS eyes

**eence** once

**eeran** → NORTH EAST **tae rin an eeran** to go shopping, to do the shopping

**eerans** NORTH EAST shopping

**eese** NORTH EAST use

    **nae eese ava** no use at all

**effeiring to** LEGAL SCOTS pertaining to

**efter** after
    **see you efter** after what? after nothing; just means *see you later, see you*

**efterneen** NORTH EAST afternoon

**Embra** the capital city of Scotland

**erra** GLASGOW rendering of *there's a*
    **erra wee way to go yet** there's quite a way to go yet

**erse** NORTH EAST arse
    **ah couldna be ersed** SLANG I couldn't be bothered, couldn't be arsed

**ess** NORTH EAST SHETLAND ashes

**essikert** SHETLAND refuse vehicle, bin lorry

**expede** LEGAL SCOTS draw up

**eywis** always

# Ff

**fa** NORTH EAST who

**factor** LEGAL SCOTS Some Scottish flats have a manager or a company who is paid to look after repairs, painting of common parts etc. This **factor** tends to have a reputation for not getting things done.

**fae** NORTH EAST from

**fæder** SHETLAND father

**Fair** The last two weeks in July in Glasgow are known as the **Fair**. It's a traditional time for holidays (especially in the older industrial days).

**fairly that** NORTH EAST right enough

**fairm** farm

**fairmer** farmer

**fairt** SHETLAND scared

**faither** father

**fan** NORTH EAST when

**fancy piece** NORTH EAST

> In the North East of Scotland a woman wouldn't be at all bothered about her man having a **fancy piece**. She might even offer him one. It's a cake.

**fankle** mess; tangle
**yer cables are all fankled up** your cables are all tangled up

> he got himself into a right fankle with question 3 in his maths test

**fantoosh** OLDER SCOTS flashy

**far**[1] NORTH EAST where

**far ye fae?** where are you from?

**far**[2] → **I could see her far enough** I can't stand her; I can't be bothered with her

**fash** bother, upset

**dinna fash yersel** This has differing shades of meaning: don't worry about it; don't get angry, don't be annoyed

**Fatty Corner** This is the crossroads of Argyle Street and Union Street in Glasgow, currently providing fast food outlets on all four corners.

**feart** afraid

**feartie** coward

**fecht** OLDER SCOTS fight

**feck** NORTH EAST OLDER SCOTS majority

**feel** NORTH EAST This is also used as an adjective: *daft, silly*. Or as a noun: *fool*.

**fell** highly

**fell muckle** OLDER SCOTS enormous

**fend** NORTH EAST effort, attempt

**fergie** combine harvester (because made by Massey Ferguson)

**fey** OLDER SCOTS [pronounced FAY] doomed

**fi** from

**ficher** NORTH EAST OLDER SCOTS tinker, fiddle

> **ah'll hae a ficher aboot wi the engine and have it fixed in no time**

**fiere** OLDER SCOTS friend

**fin** NORTH EAST when (*conjunction, for indirect questions*)

**find** → **she didn't have her troubles to find** she had a lot of troubles, she wasn't short of troubles

**fine** NORTH EAST

> This has a slightly different usage in Aberdeenshire – it is much more positive. If you ask someone whether they enjoyed their day off and they reply that **it was fine**, that means that it was lovely rather than just OK.
> **she's a fine quine** This is most commonly used to mean *she's a friendly woman.*

**fine well** very well

> **you know fine well what I mean**

> **first-foot** To **first-foot** someone is to visit them first thing in the New Year, maybe just after midnight or maybe a little later, on New Year's Day. First-footers will traditionally be made welcome and given a drink or two. This custom is nowadays less common than it was.

> **let's go round and first-foot the Macleods**

**fiscal** LEGAL SCOTS short for **procurator fiscal**, a Scottish public prosecutor

> **fish supper** fish and chips. It's not usual in Scotland to specify the type of fish or to offer a choice. If you want fish without the chips, ask for a **single fish**.

**fistle** NORTH EAST rummage

**fit¹** NORTH EAST what

**fit²** → NORTH EAST **fit like?** how are you?
**fit ye daein?** what are you doing?
**fit div ye wint?** what do you want?

**fit wye** NORTH EAST 1) why 2) how
   **fit wye nae?** why not?
   **fit a stoater!** that's brilliant!
   **fit wye can I help you?** how can I help you?

**fitba** football

**fitna een** NORTH EAST which one

**fizz** → **he had a face like fizz** he looked very angry

**flair** floor

**flechie** NORTH EAST flea-bitten

**flee** SHETLAND fishing fly

**fleein** SLANG drunk

**fleg** NORTH EAST startle; scare

**flit** move house (*also Northern English*)

**flite** scold

**flitting** move (from one home to another)

**flooer** flower

> **Flower of Scotland** This song, written by Roy
> Williamson of The Corries, has taken on the status of
> Scotland's national anthem, though not officially yet
> (2016). Most Scots, especially sporting ones, will know
> the words sung to the stirringly mournful tune. Here's
> the first verse:
>
>> O Flower of Scotland,
>> When will we see
>> Your like again,
>> That fought and died for,
>> Your wee bit Hill and Glen,

And stood against him,
Proud Edward's Army,
And sent him homeward,
Tae think again.

© *The Corries (Music) Ltd*

**flunky** SLANG condom

**fly** NORTH EAST same as a **fly cup**

**fly cup** NORTH EAST cup of tea or coffee; the word **fly** no longer has any separate meaning; the cup of tea or coffee will be neither quick nor taken in a furtive manner

**fly half** a quick half pint of beer (as well as the rugby position)

**flyting** quarrel; slanging match

**foo** NORTH EAST how
  **foo mony?** how many?
  **foo ye daein'?** how are you doing?
  **foo aul are ye?** how old are you?

**fool** NORTH EAST In the North East this can also mean *dirty*.

**fool mochit** NORTH EAST filthy dirty

**foosty** 1) smelly, like an old room
  2) NORTH EAST mouldy

**footer** fiddle

> **painting in behind the pipes is a terrible footer**

**footery** fiddly

**for** → **what are ye for?** what would you like?, as said in a bar, for example

**forby(e)** OLDER SCOTS also; besides
  **forby(e) that** moreover; apart from that

**forenoon** late morning

**forfochen** OLDER SCOTS done in, exhausted

**forjeskit** exhausted

**forkietail** SHETLAND NORTH EAST earwig

**fou** OLDER SCOTS drunk

**foushty, fousty** NORTH EAST mouldy

**fowk** NORTH EAST people, folk

**foy** SHETLAND party

> **Fringe** An annual Edinburgh arts festival
> which takes place over 3 weeks in August/September,
> attracting thousands of performers from all over the
> UK and abroad, who stage shows of all conceivable
> types in venues large and small.

**frush** NORTH EAST OLDER SCOTS tender, sensitive

**fu** 1) full 2) drunk 3) NORTH EAST how
  **fu is du?** SHETLAND how are you?

**fud** SLANG 1) a three-letter word for female parts
  2) also used as a term of abuse

> **not that one, ya fud!**

**fuil** NORTH EAST fool
  **gang fuil** go crazy

**fur** rendering of *for*

**fur coat n nae knickers** all for show, superficial, flashy

**furth of** outside

> **the Burns museum lies furth of the capital city**

**fyles** NORTH EAST sometimes

# Gg

**gad!** NORTH EAST yuck!

**gadge** SLANG guy

    **the ticket gadge** the ticket man

**gadgie** NORTH EAST man, guy

    **a gallus wee gadgie** a tough little character

**gads!** NORTH EAST yuck!

**gaed** NORTH EAST gave; given

**Gaelic** [pronounced GALLIC] Scots Gaelic is closely related to Irish and more distantly to Welsh and has an estimated 60,000 speakers (out of a total Scottish population of some 5.25 million). Place name evidence suggests that at least some Gaelic was once spoken all over Scotland, probably between 500 and 1000 AD, but it was gradually ousted by the Scots language spoken in and around the developing capital of Edinburgh. In the later Middle Ages, the language became increasingly identified with the West Highlands and Western Isles. These are the main Gaelic-speaking parts of Scotland today. All over Scotland you will find road signs in English and Gaelic, television and radio offer Gaelic programmes, and there are a number of schools offering Gaelic Medium Education. But there's a way to go yet before Gaelic is anything like a second language in Scotland and even in communities where Gaelic is the main language you won't come across anyone who is not bilingual in English. Some basic Gaelic phrases are given on pages 152-153.

**gaet** SHETLAND path

**gallus** 1) tough 2) cocky 3) brilliant, great

**galluses** braces (*for trousers*)

**gammon** the same as *ham* in England

**gan** NORTH EAST going

   **hud gan** keep going

**gang** OLDER SCOTS go

**gansey** SHETLAND jersey

**gash** SLANG rubbish, crap

**gaun** 1) going 2) go on
   **gaun yersel!** SLANG go on!, go for it!

**geggie** SLANG mouth

   **shut yer geggie** shut your mouth

**gemme** [pronounced GAME] game

**gemmie** SLANG brilliant

**gen up?** SLANG is that right?

**Gers** Rangers football team

**get** → **I'll get you down the road** not a threat, this means I'll walk down the road with you

**gey** [pronounced GUY] very

   **gey cauld the nicht, eh?** pretty cold tonight, eh?

**ghillie shoes** traditional leather shoes worn with the kilt

**gie** give

**gies** give us

   **dinnae gies that crap** don't give us that crap

**gieza...** can I have...?

> This is a common way of asking for something in a shop or bar; it sounds abrupt to the non-Scots ear but isn't perceived as rude.

**gin** OLDER SCOTS if; you're only likely to come across this nowadays in songs or poems

**ging** NORTH EAST go

**ginger** GLASGOW any fizzy soft drink

**girdle** griddle; for cooking pancakes and the like on

**girn** whine

**girnie** Someone who is **girnie** is alway whining about something. It's often used for a baby, who just feels like a good whine about things.

**girse** NORTH EAST grass

**glaikit** stupid, gormless

**Glasgow** Scotland's largest city with an industrial heritage of heavy engineering and shipbuilding on the Clyde and trade with the colonies in the late 18th century, notably the importation of tobacco and sugar. Despite a decline in heavy industry, the city has experienced a revival in fortunes and is now a major retail and business centre with a highly developed sense of self-promotion. A place where people talk to people.

**Glasgow Fair** This is a traditional two-week July holiday in Glasgow, when factories would shut and you'd take your holidays then (whether it suited or no).

**glaur** [pronounced to rhyme with FLOOR] mud

**gleikit** same as **glaikit**

**Glencoe** In 1691 the government of William and Mary demanded that **Jacobite** clan chiefs sign an oath of allegiance. The chief of the Macdonalds of Glencoe was late in doing so and this was seen as a pretext for action against them. A regiment belonging to the  →

Campbell Earl of Argyll was dispatched to Glencoe where the Macdonalds were obliged to offer them hospitality. Shortly afterwards the commander of the regiment received orders that all Macdonalds under 70 were to be put to the sword. The massacre took place in February 1692. Thirty-eight of the clan were killed, including the chief, and more died trying to escape over the mountains. This massacre has gone down in history as the Campbells wreaking revenge on their old enemies the Macdonalds when in fact they were following orders which came from the King himself.

**glengarry** a type of cap with a fold at the top running front to back and two strands of cloth hanging down at the back

**Glesca** Glasgow

**Glesca screwdriver** a hammer

*a couple of glengarries*

*just a wee Glesga kiss*

**Glesga** Glasgow

**Glesga kiss** a head butt

**Glesgie** Glasgow

**gloaming** dusk

**glottal stop**

> This is the characteristically Glaswegian omission of the
> 't' sound, making **buh-uh** out of *butter* and **beh-uh**
> out of *better*.

**gluff** SHETLAND fright

**go** can also mean *ride*
  **he nivver learnt tae go a bike** he never learned to ride a bike

**goat** rendering of *got*

**goldie** → **a wee goldie** an affectionate expression for a
  glass of whisky

**gonna, gonnae** going to

> Also used to form typically Glaswegian requests.
> **gonnae gieza a fiver?** can you give me a fiver?
> **gonnae no say that!** please don't say that

**goonie** gown, nightdress

**gooser** NORTH EAST gooseberry

**gow** NORTH EAST OLDER SCOTS gull

**gowk** cuckoo

**Graham** any Scottish mountain between 2,000 feet and 2,500 feet (610-762m)

**grain** SHETLAND small amount

**graip** NORTH EAST fork, garden fork

**graith** OLDER SCOTS gear, tools, tackle; things

**Granite City** → **the Granite City** Aberdeen

**gravat** scarf

**Great Glen** This is the name given to the rift valley which runs from Inverness on the east coast to Fort William on the west coast. In 1822 the Caledonian Canal was built through the glen linking the Lochs Ness, Oich and Lochy and providing a navigable waterway from one side of Scotland to the other.

**greet**

> Also means *cry, weep*
> **ach, dinna greet, hen, he'll be back**
> **ah jist went hame n had a good greet**

**greeter** someone who cries a lot; a cry-baby

**greetin face** SLANG jocular, but not terribly respectful, form of address. As seen at **bawface**, the Scots are fond of terms alluding to the shape and look of a person's face. **hey, greetin face, giezat hammer willya** hey, chum, pass that hammer, eh?

**greit** same as **greet**

**greive** head farmworker

**Gretna Green** Just over the border from England, this small town became famous as the romantic destination for eloping couples trying to escape the tighter English marriage laws. Originally, in Scotland, a man and woman over the age of 16 could be married simply by declaring themselves husband and wife in front of witnesses. Nowadays a minister or authorized registrar must officiate but there are no stipulations regarding residence in the country and no parental consent is required for couples over 16.

**grind** SHETLAND gate

**grip** → NORTH EAST **he's such a grip** he's so tight with his money

**grippie** NORTH EAST tight, stingy, mean

**growler** NORTH EAST SLANG an ugly-looking woman; an old bag

**grun** NORTH EAST ground

**gubbing** defeat, often in a sports context

> **the under 15s got a right gubbing on Sunday, 35-3**

**gubful** mouthful

**guddle** mess

> **seen his desk? what a guddle!**

**gude** OLDER SCOTS good

**guff** NORTH EAST an English person

**guffie** NORTH EAST This is an English person. Either because of the Cockney habit of calling people *guv* or because of a tendency to talk a load of guff. Or maybe both.

**guid** good

**guid...** OLDER SCOTS ...in-law

**guid kens** SHETLAND god knows

**guidman** OLDER SCOTS husband

**guiser** A person, normally a child, who goes out **guising** at Halloween. The term also has special meaning at the annual **Up-Helly-Aa** festival. It involves squads of guisers parading around Lerwick, performing skits in the local halls, the burning of a replica Viking longship and general mayhem. The most important person in all this is the "Guiser Jarl" who leads the "Jarl Squad" who are all very elaborately dressed up as Vikings.

**guising** At Halloween children go out from door to door dressed up as witches, pirates, cowboys, James Bond or anything you like, and, if invited in to a house, which is the custom, sing a song or tell a funny story, in exchange for some sweets or a little cash. Most people will have a special store of sweets and chocolate laid out in anticipation of the guising.

**guizer** same as **guiser**

**guttered** SLANG drunk

**gutties** trainers

**gye** same as **gey**

**gype** NORTH EAST SLANG idiot

# Hh

**haar** EAST COAST sea mist

**hacker** NORTH EAST As well as the standard meaning of a
*computer hacker* this can also be
1) a smelly or repulsive person
2) an aggressive person.

**hackit** 1) ugly 2) NORTH EAST smelly, repulsive

**haddy** 1) fool, twit 2) short for haddock

**haggis supper** go to the **Menu Reader**

**haill** whole

**haillie** wholly

**hairst** SHETLAND autumn

**hairy (Mary)** GLASGOW a young girl, from teens to early
twenties; a **hairy** is not going to be posh, it's not a
flattering term

**hak** NORTH EAST search

> hakkin aroon in the gorse for his golf ba

**hale jing bang** NORTH EAST the whole lot

**hale** → NORTH EAST **it's hale watter** it's bucketing down,
it's pouring with rain

**half and half** half a pint of beer and a whisky

**ham-and-egger** NORTH EAST SLANG an incompetent,
useless person

**Hampden** also **Hampden Park**, an international stadium
(for football or rugby) in Glasgow

**hand** → NORTH EAST **to draw through hand** to go over, to
talk over

**happit** covered

**harl** NORTH EAST To **harl** a wall is to roughcast it.

**harling** NORTH EAST roughcast

**hashed** NORTH EAST SLANG busy; in a hurry
**ah'm gye hashed the day** I'm very busy today
**I cannae talk the noo, I'm hashed** can't talk now, I'm in a rush

**haud** hold

**hauf** half
**a wee hauf** a whisky

**haugh** IN PLACE NAMES a meadow by a river, from the Old English *healh* or *halh* meaning *corner* or *nook*. So: **Fleshers' Haugh** (on Glasgow Green, where Rangers first played).

**haun** hand

**haver** [pronounced to rhyme with SHAVER] talk nonsense; dither
**what's he havering aboot?** what's he drivelling on about?

**Haymarket** → **getting off at the Haymarket** SLANG Haymarket is the first railway station as you come into Edinburgh; the next stop, Waverley, is as far as you can go. So, in the Scots vernacular, getting off at the Haymarket is coitus interruptus.

**head** → **you'll have your head in your hands to play with** you'll be in trouble

**heather** → **it won't exactly set the heather alight** it won't cause much of a sensation; a phrase about as much used as the English equivalent: *it won't exactly set the Thames on fire.*

**heavy** This type of beer is the closest thing to English bitter and is what you should ask for if you want to sound more like a native.

**heavy** GLASGOW SLANG absolutely, totally

> **I'm heavy serious, man**

**heedrum hodrum** A mocking term used by Scots to describe traditional Scottish music, the sort of music of which they are not fans; the word is also used to refer to the Gaelic language or (in the plural) to Gaelic speakers.

**hee-haw** a euphemistic expression emphasizing the negative:
1) not at all, absolutely not
2) nothing
**ye can sing hee-haw** you can't sing at all

**heelie** the crust or end piece of a loaf

**heenies awa** NORTH EAST a long time ago; a long way away

**hegri** SHETLAND heron

**heid** [pronounced HEED] head

**heid-banger** SLANG nutter, crazy person

**heid-nip** → SLANG **it's a real heid-nip** it really does my head in; I can't stand it

**Heilander** Highlander

**Heilandman's umbrella** At Glasgow's Central Station, the railway bridge as it spans Argyle Street.

**hell** → **hell mend her!** to hell with her!

**hems** → **to put the hems on** to ruin, to put an end to, to do away with

**hen** Used in the Glasgow area as a form of address to a woman, either an acquaintance or a stranger, this is the female equivalent of **Jimmy**.
**is that your bag ye left there, hen?**

**het¹** In a children's game of tag or tig **het** is the kid who has been caught and who now has to chase the others. (Normally called *it* in Southern English).

**het²** NORTH EAST hot

**heuch** NORTH EAST 1) cliff 2) ravine

**heuchter-teuchter** A word used in a mocking and derogatory way by Scots to refer to the sort of stereotypically Scottish things they don't think much of, like **heuchter-teuchter music** or **heuchter-teuchter dancing**.

**High Court of Justiciary** LEGAL SCOTS the supreme criminal court

**high doh** go to **doh**

**high heid yin** [pronounced high-HEED-yun]
1) boss
2) important person, VIP

**Higher** This is an examination which is taken at the end of the fifth or sixth year at a Scottish school at the age of 16 or 17. Although the exam is taken at an earlier age than English A levels, Scottish kids normally take a wider range of Highers than English kids do at A level. After **Highers** there is the option of taking Advanced Highers.

**Highland Games** Highland games are spectacles that combine music and sport. You'll get tossing the caber, highland dancing, pipe bands, beer tents etc. They can be traced back to the days when clan chiefs would audition to find the strongest warriors and best entertainers for their court.

**Highland line** an imaginary line dividing the Highlands of Scotland from the Lowlands and running from the Moray Firth to the Clyde Estuary

**hine** NORTH EAST far
**hine awa** far away
**he bides hine roon the corner** he lives a long way away (North East Scots has an opposite of 'just round the corner')
**hine doon the road** right down the road

**hing** GLASGOW thing

**they're daein this karaoke hing the noo arra pub**

**hingen** NORTH EAST SLANG disgusting

**hingy** SLANG [pronounced to rhyme with CLINGY] unwell, under the weather

**hinna** NORTH EAST haven't

**hirays, hireys** EAST COAST SLANG money

**hirple** SHETLAND NORTH EAST limp; hobble

**hiv** NORTH EAST have

**hoa(t)ch** → **to hoach with something** to crawl with something, to be swarming with something

**hoa(t)ching** swarming, very busy

**Hogmanay** This is the Scottish New Year which is, some would say, more of a festival than Christmas. New Year celebrations held throughout Scotland include street parties, the biggest and best known of which is in Edinburgh, as well as **ceilidhs** and fireworks.

**holm** IN PLACE NAMES from the Old Norse *holmr* meaning *little island*. So **Lamb Holm** (a small island in Orkney).

**holograph** LEGAL SCOTS A legal document is **holograph** if entirely written in the writer's own handwriting. It does not require a witness' signature.

**Holyrood (Palace)** Holyrood Palace, at the foot of the **Royal Mile** in Edinburgh, was formerly the principal residence of the Scottish monarchs, and is now the official residence of the British monarch in Scotland. It was founded as an abbey in the 12th century, extended as a palace under James IV, and attained its present appearance in the early 1680s under Charles II.

**Holyrood (Parliament)** In 1999 the Scottish parliament was re-established after a lapse of 292 years. The new parliament building at the foot of the **Royal Mile**, a source of great controversy because of the extent to which it exceeded its original budget and timescale for completion, opened in October 2004. Certain matters (such as defence and economic policy) have been reserved to the UK parliament in Westminster.

**homer** If someone offers to do a job for you as a **homer**, then he'll be doing it in his own time, not his company's, and will expect cash for the work done.

**Honours of Scotland** This is the alternative name for the Scottish Crown Jewels (consisting of the crown, sceptre and sword of state) which are on display in the Crown Room of Edinburgh Castle along with the **Stone of Destiny**.

**hoodie** as well as someone wearing a **hoodie**, this is also a hooded crow

**hoof** → **to pad the hoof** to walk, to hoof it

**hoojigapiv** NORTH EAST OLDER SCOTS thingummyjig, whatsit

**hoolet** OLDER SCOTS an owl

**hoose** house

**hornie** EAST COAST SLANG policeman
   **the hornies** the police

**horse into** NORTH EAST To **horse into** food is to get stuck
   into it with enthusiasm.

**host** SHETLAND cough

**houghmagandie** sexual cavorting, a humorous or
   calvinistically humorless term

**how**

> In Scotland this can, confusingly for others, also mean *why*.
> **I don't love you any more – how?** baffling to the
> English ear
> **I stopped him going out – how?** confusion here; is
> it the means or the reason that's being asked about?;
> context will normally decide

**Howe** IN PLACE NAMES low-lying ground. So: **Howe of Fife**:
   Fife valley.

**howf(f)** OLDER SCOTS A shelter or meeting place, this older
   word is still found in pub names like Burns' Howff and
   can be used to mean a rough pub, a dive. The hut on a
   building site might also be known as a **howff**.

**howk** dig

**huddery** scruffy

**hudgie** a ride taken by hanging on the back of a van etc

> **ah'll gie ye a hudgie on ma bike**

**huff** → **in the huff** English would be: in a huff

**hunner** NORTH EAST hundred

**hurdies** NORTH EAST bottom, hips

> **you'll get a breeze up your hurdies wearing a kilt!**

**hurl** a lift in a car; a car ride

> **ah'll gie ye a hurl doon the road, hen**

**hytering and skytering** NORTH EAST stumbling, though
the Scots paints a livelier picture of limbs flying about in
all directions in an attempt not to hit the deck.

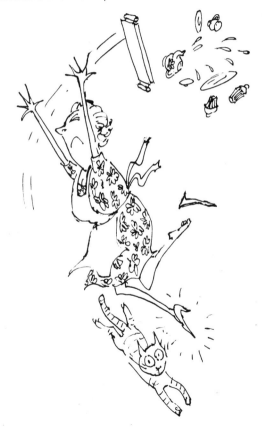

# Ii

**Ibrox** the home of Glasgow Rangers

**icicle** NORTH EAST This can also mean an *ice lolly*.

**idjit** idiot

**-ie** This suffix is very widespread in Scots, particularly in the North East. As with its continental counterparts (like -chen, -lein, in German, -(t)je in Dutch) it connotes not merely smallness, but expresses an affectionate attitude on the part of the speaker. Some examples: **mannie**; **wifie**; **laddie**; **gadgie**.

**ilk** → **of that ilk** If you happen to meet someone called, say, **Alan Dunmuir of that ilk**, then you have met someone who comes from a place called Dunmuir and who is also the **laird** or owner of that place.

**ilka, ilky** NORTH EAST OLDER SCOTS each; every

**Immortal Memory** The Immortal Memory is the name given to a speech made at more formal **Burns suppers**, the subject matter being some aspect of Burns' life or poetry.

**inaneth** NORTH EAST OLDER SCOTS under

**inby** OLDER SCOTS inside (*a building*)

**inch** IN PLACE NAMES from the Gaelic *innis* meaning *island*. So **Inchcolm**: St Columba's Isle.

**Int2** If you hear a Scot talking about doing Int2s then the reference is to school exams at a level between **Standard Grade** and **Highers**.

**intae** NORTH EAST This is sometimes used in place of *in*.
**living intae anither place** living in another place
**nae lowdy intae his pooch** no money in his pocket

**interdict** LEGAL SCOTS injunction, banning order

**intimations** You may see this as a heading in a newspaper. The English equivalent would be *Births, Marriages and Deaths*.

**inver** IN PLACE NAMES from the Gaelic ***inbhir*** meaning *river mouth*. So **Inverness**: Nessmouth.

**Iona Abbey** In 563 AD St Columba founded a Celtic monastery on this little island off the west coast of Scotland. Through the centuries Iona became a place of pilgrimage and a burial place for kings (Scottish, Norwegian and Irish). In the middle ages a Benedictine abbey and a nunnery were built here. The abbey was restored early last century and this peaceful little island still attracts visitors from all over the world.

**Irn Bru®** go to the **Menu Reader** on page 147

**is**

> 1) In Scots the verb form **is** can be used with plural subjects, apart from the personal subjects *we, you* and *they*.
> **the new glasses is all broken**
>
> 2) In the North East you'll hear **is it** used as an equivalent of *isn't it*.
> **it's a fine day, is it?**

**-it** In Scots this ending corresponds to -ed.

> **that's the fuel pump sortit**

**ither** other

# Jj

J can also be pronounced JAI to rhyme with SPY or HIGH, but only when saying the alphabet or spelling a word.

**Jacobites** The name deriving from the Latin for James (*Jacobus*) was given to the supporters of James VII (and subsequently James Francis Edward Stewart and Bonnie Prince Charlie) who wanted to see the Stewart monarchy restored to the throne. Several uprisings took place between 1689 and 1746 with varying degrees of success. Final defeat came at the battle of **Culloden**. Subsequent measures ensured that no future Jacobite rebellions would occur and dramatically reduced the power of the **clan system**.

**jag** injection

**Jags** a nickname for Partick Thistle Football Club

**jaikit** jacket

**jake** SLANG an idiot, a general term of abuse, shortened from **jakey**

**jakey** SLANG a down-and-out

> aye, and wan of thae jakeys used tae be a surgeon, so they say

**jalouse** NORTH EAST conclude; guess, suppose

**Jambos** a nickname for Heart of Midlothian football team, Hearts

**jammy piece** a jam sandwich

**jannie** janitor

**jap** splash

**jawbox** OLDER SCOTS kitchen sink (there is a Scots word to *jaw* which means to *pour* or to *splash*)

**jeely** 1) NORTH EAST jelly 2) jam

**jeely piece** a jam sandwich, not so common these days, but a standard snack in the early to mid 20th century

**jeezo!** SLANG a fairly mild exclamation, like *heavens* or *crikey*

**jessie** SLANG an effeminate man (also used in the North of England)

**jiggered** exhausted, knackered

**Jimmy** GLASGOW A form of address for any man. This is often shortened to **Jim**. Unlike its female counterpart, **hen**, the word would not normally be used between two men who know each other.

**gonnae move yer van there, Jim?** can you move your van, mate

**jiner** joiner

**jingbang** → **the whole jingbang** the whole lot, the whole caboodle

**jings!** good heavens!

**jist** just

**Jock Tamson's bairns** → **we're a' Jock Tamson's bairns** we're all on this planet together and none of us is inherently any more or less deserving than another, we're all God's little children

**Joe Baxi** RHYMING SLANG taxi

**jooks** same as **jukes**

**jorrie** OLDER SCOTS marble, the sort kids used to play with

**josser** → **auld josser** old bloke

**jotter** At school a **jotter** is an exercise book.

> **if she carries on like that, she'll be getting her jotters** she'll get the sack

**jouk** dodge

**jukes** To put or hide something **up your jukes** means to put or hide it up the front of your clothing.

**jungle** → GLASGOW **The Jungle** is a nickname for the Celtic end at Celtic's home ground, Parkhead.

# Kk

**kaim** NORTH EAST OLDER SCOTS comb

**keech** excrement, crap

**keek** look, peek

> **keek!** Scots wifies say **keek** to wee babies, while English ones go *peekaboo!*

**keeker** black eye

**keelie** the stereotypical Glaswegian, tough and defiant and working class

**keks** SLANG underpants

**Kelpie** In Scottish folklore a kelpie is a water demon, usually taking the form of a horse, which lures humans into the water in order to drown them and eat them.

**Kelvinside** A posh part of Glasgow, seen as posh particularly because of the (supposed) accent of its inhabitants; this is where *sex* refers to things you keep potatoes in and where a *crèche* is an accident between two motor vehicles. Parallel to **Morningside** in Edinburgh.

**ken** EAST COAST know
**dinna ken** don't know

> This is also used as a filler word.
> **I cannae face seeing her again, ken?** ...know what I mean?
> **it'll be round here somewhere, ken**
> it'll be round here somewhere, right

**kenspeckle** distinctive; prominent; well-known

**kent** known

**kil** IN PLACE NAMES from the Gaelic *cill* meaning *church*. So **Kilmarnock**: church of St Marnock.

**Killie** a nickname for Kilmarnock football team

**kilt** If a Scot is going to wear a kilt (and not all do) then it is most likely to be for a special occasion like a wedding, a graduation ceremony or maybe an international rugby match.

**kiltie** an informal way of referring to a man wearing a kilt

**kin¹** can

**kin²** IN PLACE NAMES from the Gaelic *ceann* meaning *head*. So **Kingussie**: head of the pinewood; **Kinlochleven**: head of Loch Leven.

**kine** cows, cattle

**kinna** kind of

**kirk** church

**Hector, why so alone? come into the body of the kirk** come and join the main group; come and join us (*there is no religious connotation to this idiom*)

**kirn** 1) churn 2) NORTH EAST In the North East this can also be used to mean a *mess*

**kist** NORTH EAST OLDER SCOTS chest, storage box

**kitchie deem** NORTH EAST kitchen girl

**kite** SLANG same as **kyte**

**klype** tell tales. Also a noun.

the wee klype has telt the teacher

**knacked** 1) broken 2) done in; knackered

**knock** IN PLACE NAMES from the Gaelic ***cnoc*** meaning *hill* (although the pronunciation has been anglicized, the Gaelic being pronounced CROC). So **Knockbain**: white hill.

**knock back** refuse, reject

**knot** → **she was fair knotting herself** she was laughing her head off

**knowe** IN PLACE NAMES from the Old Norse ***knoll-r*** meaning *hilltop*.

**knype on** NORTH EAST [pronounced NIP] hurry up

**kye** cattle

**kyle** IN PLACE NAMES from the Gaelic ***caol*** meaning *strait*

> **the Waverley, the world's last remaining sea-going paddle steamer, took us around the Kyles of Bute**

**kypie** NORTH EAST head

**kyte** SLANG belly
**up the kyte** pregnant

**kythe** OLDER SCOTS appear

# Ll

**labdick** SLANG policeman

**laekit** → SHETLAND **weel laekit** well liked

**laich** IN PLACE NAMES lower; survives in names such **The Laich Hall** (*of a castle*). In lowland Scots a *laich* is a stretch of low-lying ground. **The Lake of Menteith** was originally the Laich of Menteith.

**laird** landowner; similar to a lord of the manor

**laldy**

> A range of related uses.
> **to get laldy** to get into trouble, to get a telling off
> **he'll be getting laldy when he gets home**
> **give it laldy** really go for it
> **in the second half of the gig the band really gave it laldy**
> **the couple in the hotel room next door were giving it laldy**
> **he gave him laldy** he gave him a good beating

**Lallans** Another name for Lowland Scots, the word is also used to describe a largely artificial variety of Scots concocted by the poet Hugh McDiarmid, a language that has great force of expression, but is no real mirror of spoken linguistic reality.

**lam** → **have a lam on** SLANG be annoyed, be pissed off

**lane** alone
   **I cudnae gae ma lane** I couldn't go alone

**lang** long

**langsome** NORTH EAST OLDER SCOTS boring

**larick** NORTH EAST OLDER SCOTS larch

**later** → **see you later**

> The Scots don't tend to distinguish between saying
> goodbye or cheerio to you and arranging to meet up
> with you later on. **See you later** just means *cheerio* in
> Scots. More literal-minded Sassenachs must beware of
> replying 'when?'

**lave** NORTH EAST OLDER SCOTS rest, remainder

**laverock** NORTH EAST OLDER SCOTS lark (*the feathered type*)

**law** IN PLACE NAMES hill

**leader-aff** GLASGOW gang leader

**learin** NORTH EAST education

**leck** IN PLACE NAMES from the Gaelic *leac* meaning *flat stone*
or a *slope of flat stones*. So **Lechkine**: place of flat stones;
**Auchinleck**: field of the flat stones.

**lee** NORTH EAST a lie

**leet** list

**leid** [pronounced LEED] a rather formal word for
language

> **the auld Scots leid**

**len** NORTH EAST loan
**tak a len of someone** to take advantage of someone

**lether** NORTH EAST ladder

> **licensed grocer** It's not that there are both official,
> respectable grocers and illegally operating bootleg
> grocers in Scotland, but that a licensed grocer is able to
> sell alcohol.

**lift** OLDER SCOTS sky

# like

> There are some distinctly Scots uses.
>
> 1) **like aat** SLANG like that. This is the Scots variant of a modern innovation used when relating events, either to introduce what somebody said or as a reaction to something that was said or that happened. In the latter case it is followed by an unmistakable facial expression, from which the listener will appreciate the emotion of the speaker.
>
> > **so he says, is that yur friend or yur ma yuh've brought wi yuh? n ah wuz like aat – cheeky wee bugger, so yuh are**
> >
> > **he asks me up to his place, ah wuz like aat** *(facial expression to match)*
>
> 2) **what like's the food?** a common Scots inversion. English would say: what's the food like?
>
> 3) **what'm I like!** silly me!
>
> > **what's he like, eh?** isn't he a character, eh?; can be said either in amusement or frustration
>
> 4) **likes, likesay** a filler, used to make a pause in a stream of speech; similar in use to *you know*

**links¹** sausages

**links²** NORTH EAST the area of sand dunes going down to the shore

**linn** IN PLACE NAMES from Gaelic **linn** meaning *pool.* So **Linn of Dee**: pool of the river Dee.

**lippen** trust, rely on

**loan** lane

**loch** is a Gaelic word meaning *lake.* In Scots pronunciation this word does not rhyme with *lock.*

**lochan** small loch

**Loch Awe** OLDER SCOTS → **it's a far cry from/to Loch Awe** it's very remote/a long way away

**Loch Lomond** Not quite Scotland's longest loch (at 22.6 miles or 36.2km it's slightly shorter than Lochs Awe and Ness) but it is the largest expanse of water in Britain.

**loon** NORTH EAST boy

**loons** SLANG trousers

**Lord Advocate** LEGAL SCOTS the senior law officer in Scotland

**Lord Provost** In Glasgow, Edinburgh, Aberdeen and Dundee the **Lord Provost** is the mayor.

**loun** NORTH EAST boy

**loup** NORTH EAST jump

**loupin** 1) painful
    **ma heid's loupin** my head's killing me
    2) disgusting, revolting
    **the lager's loupin** the lager's disgusting
    3) crawling, infested
    **the city centre's loupin with tourists**

**lowdy** NORTH EAST money

**loweing** glowing

**lowp** same as **loup**

**lum** chimney
    **lang may yer lum reek** literally: long may your chimney smoke, so: good luck to you, have a long and successful life

**lumber** SLANG pick-up
    **get a lumber** pick up a girl (or a boy)
    **oot looking furra lumber**

# Mm

**ma** my

**maalie** SHETLAND fulmar

**Mac..., Mc...** The common prefix in Scots surnames is from the Gaelic word meaning *son*. (In Gaelic a woman's surname has the prefix **nic**, meaning *daughter*.)

**machair** low, grassy land at the back of beaches, particularly on the Western Isles

**maddy** crazy person, can be an affectionate term

**maet** SHETLAND food

**mair** more

**mairrit** married

**maist** most

*a maalie*

**mak** make

**makar** a Scots poet laureate

**malky** razor (*as a weapon*)

**man**

> **my man** This would sound absurdly antiquated or class-ridden if spoken with an English (southern) accent; but in the Glasgow area (spoken: ma man) it's pally.

**mannie** NORTH EAST just means *man*

> **we waited at the garage for the mannie to find the loo keys**

**manse** vicarage

**manto** EAST COAST SLANG chicks, women
   **the manto's hoachin** there are chicks everywhere

**mantovani** RHYMING SLANG (= *fanny*) chicks, women, totty

> **Marches** → **Riding the Marches** A ceremony in Borders towns when horsemen patrol the boundaries of common land (known as **marches**).

**maroc** SLANG drunk

**mart day** NORTH EAST market day

**masel** myself

**maucht** NORTH EAST OLDER SCOTS effort, attempt

**maun** must

**mavis** a thrush (*a rather literary word*)

**maw** mother

**mebbe** maybe

**meen** NORTH EAST moon

**mercat** OLDER SCOTS market

**merry dancers** SHETLAND the Northern Lights, the Aurora Borealis

**messages** also: shopping, usually groceries

> I had that many messages I decided to get a taxi

**mibbe** maybe

**michty (me)!** NORTH EAST good heavens!

**mickle** → **mony a mickle maks a muckle** might be said, for example, to someone who contributes a small amount to a collection; lots of little bits can add up to something big

**midden** This is the place where dustbins are kept, usually around the back of a **tenement** block. It can also be a *rubbish tip* or, out in the country, a *dung heap*. There are of course extended uses:
**seen their office?, what a midden!**

**midder** SHETLAND mother

**midge** A midge is a small biting flying insect, particularly common in the north and west of Scotland over the summer months (but it is making its way progressively further south). They hover around in inescapable swarms and will get up your nose, in your ears, down your collar, into your mouth. Unlike holiday-makers, midges don't like hot sunshine. So when the sun's out, you'll be safe. But in the evening, or in the drizzle, or in the early morning, when you're loading up the car, out they come. Their main human characteristic is that they are supposed to find a strong reek of garlic repellent.

**midgie** 1) same as **midge** 2) same as **midden**

**midgie man** a refuse collector, not to be confused with the following

**midgie raker** a down-and-out who scavenges in dustbins and litterbins

**min** NORTH EAST man; a way of addressing any male, like **mon** in older Scots.
**aricht min!** alright chum!

**mince** SLANG rubbish
**he's talking a loada mince**
**see these new cartons, pure mince** these new cartons are rubbish
**yer heid's mince** you're just not with it

**mind** also: remember
**do you mind when we...?** do you remember when we...?

**minder, mindin** a small gift; a souvenir; a New Year's present

**mines** mine

> All the other personal pronouns add an s to the possessive adjective (your/yours; our/ours etc) and Scots does the same for *mine*.

**minister** Scottish churches have ministers rather than vicars.

**mink** NORTH EAST a dirty individual, a social outcast

**mintee, mintie** NORTH EAST minute
**wait a mintie** wait a minute

**mintit** SLANG great, brilliant

**mirackle** SHETLAND injure severely

**miroclous** GLASGOW drunk (a contortion of miraculous)

**mirry dancers** SHETLAND the Northern Lights, the Aurora Borealis

**misanter** SHETLAND accident

**mischanter** NORTH EAST accident (The c is not pronounced).

**miss yourself** miss out on a good time

> **och, ye should've been there, great party, ye really missed yerself**

**missives** LEGAL SCOTS If you are buying or selling a house then the missives are all the legal documents that are drawn up relating to the sale. When *missives are concluded* then the sale is complete.

**mither** OLDER SCOTS mother

**mixter-maxter** mish-mash; a bit of this and a bit of that

**mo'uh** SLANG This book is not attempting to put all the re-articulations of accent into print. But this one is so common. If you're a traveller in Scotland, you should know that your **mo'uh**, especially if you're driving around the Glasgow area, is your car (it's also Cockney, of course).

**mochie** NORTH EAST wet, dreary and dismal

**mochit** NORTH EAST filthy

**Mod** Festival of Gaelic music held in October including singing, dancing and piping competitions. The location changes every year.

**Moderator** In the Church of Scotland the Moderator is the person elected to chair meetings of Church Assemblies.

**modren** NORTH EAST modern

**mon** NORTH EAST man; usually as an interjection

> **ye'll no find him at hame the day, mon**

**Mons Meg** a 6 ton medieval siege gun now housed in Edinburgh Castle

**mony** many

**moocher** → NORTH EAST **he's a moocher** he's always borrowing things

**moorit** SHETLAND light brown (the colour of Shetland sheep)

**moosey-faced** miserable-looking

**moothie** a mouthorgan

**more** IN PLACE NAMES from the Gaelic *mòr* meaning *big*. So **Aviemore**: big hill face.

**morn** → **the morn** tomorrow
**the morn's morn** tomorrow morning

**Morningside** A posh part of Edinburgh; the word has connotations of gentility and a Morningside accent definitely sets you aside from the hoi-polloi, this being the place where people think that *sex* is what people in olden days used to buy coal in. Similar to **Kelvinside** in Glasgow.

**morra** → GLASGOW **the morra** tomorrow

**mouth music** A technique comparable to scat in jazz or rapping without actual words, **mouth music** is nonsense words sung in imitation of the sound of the bagpipes. It originated in 1746 when playing the bagpipes was prohibited in the aftermath of **Culloden**.

**mowrie** NORTH EAST sandy shingle

**mowrie beach** NORTH EAST shingly beach

**mowser** moustache

**MSP** member of the Scottish parliament

**muckle** big; much
**nae muckle luck** not much luck

**mull** a peninsula or headland

**Munro** any Scottish mountain over 3,000 feet (914m)

**Munro-bagging** climbing Scottish mountains over 3,000
feet as a kind of collector's hobby

**Murrayfield** the home of Scottish international rugby

# Nn

**nae** no; not

**nash** EAST COAST SLANG hurry

> **goat tae nash** gotta go, gotta dash

**naw** no

**neb** SLANG nose

> **to take a neb at something** to take a look at something

**ned** yob, yobbo

> the neds keep smashing the glass at the bus stop

**neddy** yobbish

> me in a white shellsuit? ah'd just look pure neddy,
> so ah would

**nedette** a female ned

**need**

> Two distinctly Scots constructions with this verb:
>
> 1) **it needs painted/specified**
>
> The use of the past participle is normal Scots here.
> Non-Scots would use the present participle and say *it
> needs painting/specifying*.
>
> 2) a fairly complex construction:
> **you wouldnae need tae be saving yer money** it's a
> good job you're not trying to save money, it's just as
> well you're not trying to save money

**neen** NORTH EAST none

**ne'erday** New Year's Day

**neesik** SHETLAND porpoise

**neist** next

**ness** SHETLAND headland

> **Nessie** This is the name given to the Loch Ness
> Monster; there's only one name though for all the
> sightings; you'd have thought that if the loch actually
> has had a monster in it all this time, there must be at
> least two of them just so as to keep the monster family
> going...

**neuk** corner; nook

**news** NORTH EAST chat
  **he drapped in for a news** he dropped in for a chat
  **to have a bit of a news** to have a chat

**nicht** night
  **the nicht** tonight

**nickum** NORTH EAST a rascal, a mischief-maker

**nip** hurt
  **it's still nippin a wee bit, but I'll survive**
  **to nip someone's heid** to annoy someone by nagging

**nippie** NORTH EAST an informal word for a waitress

**nippie sweetie** GLASGOW a sharp-tongued person

**nippit** tight, tight-fitting

**nithing** NORTH EAST nothing

**no** also means **not**

> **will ye no stop for a wee drink?**
> **it's getting a wee bit late, is it no?**

**nocht** OLDER SCOTS nothing

**nondy** ⌐SLANG⌐ stupid

**noo** → **the noo** (right) now

> This also has the dual usage of English *just now* or *right now* referring both to the present and to a time just past.
>
> **he was sitting right there the noo**

**noost** ⌐SHETLAND⌐ a hollow on the shore where a boat is kept

**nor** In Scots this can also have the meaning of *than.*

> **mair nor that** more than that

**not**

> **you've heard him sing, have you not?**
>
> To southern English ears this is a very formal sounding construction and would be replaced in speech by *haven't you.* There is nothing formal about the Scots usage.

**notion** → **to take a notion to someone** to take a liking to someone; to fancy someone

**nyaff** 1) small or insignificant person

2) irritating, stupid, unimportant person

> **when the boss puts his old raincoat on he looks jist like a wee nyaff**
>
> **get aff the sofa and dae some decoratin, ye useless great nyaff!**

# Oo

**ocht** anything

**offie** an off-licence

> Morag, could you no stop by at the offie and pick
> up a bottle of French red and some lager for
> Willie

**offski** SLANG leaving, going, off

> 11 o'clock, time I was offski

**Old Firm game** a football match between Celtic and
Rangers. These two rival Glasgow teams are seen as a
unit, the Old Firm. Games between them tend to make
the headlines for more than sporting reasons.

**ony** [pronounced to rhyme with TONY] any

**oo** SHETLAND wool

**oor** our

**oose** fluff, dust

> there was about ten years' worth of oose under the
> bed

**oosey** fluffy, with bits of fluff coming off

> ma new sweater's gone all oosey

**oot** out

**ootay** out of

**or (eest)** NORTH EAST until

> ah'm waitressing the noo or (eest) ah find
> somethin better

**Orcadian** 1) from the Orkney Islands; 2) an inhabitant of the Orkney Islands

**orra**[1] coarse

**orra**[2] GLASGOW all the
**izzat orra weans away the noo?** have all the kids left now?

**orraman** odd-job man

**ory** dirty

**other** → **your other national drink**. All Scots will know what this refers to. It's **Irn Bru®** (go to page 147).

**outsider** In Glasgow this is more than just a sociological concept: it is also one of the two crusts of a loaf of bread, also known as a **heelie**.

**outwith** outside; outside of; beyond

> **outwith the scope of this agreement**
> **outwith normal school hours**

**ower** over
**ah'm no ower auld tae...** I'm not too old to...

**owre** over

**oxter** armpit

# Pp

**P&J (=Press and Journal)** a daily newspaper for the whole of northern Scotland

**P3, P4** etc primary 3, primary 4 etc in school

**pairk, park** also means a *field*

**pal**

> One of the most commonly used terms to address another person. But it's not always that friendly, as the tone of voice will let you know.
> **goat a light, pal?**
> **that's no very nice, pal, you need tae watch yer step**

**pan** → SLANG **to knock your pan in** to knacker or exhaust yourself

**pan loaf** → NORTH EAST **to put on the pan loaf** to try to speak with a posh accent

**panel¹** LEGAL SCOTS If a lawyer in a courtroom refers to the **panel**, then he is referring to the accused standing in the dock.

**panel²** SLANG hit, clout

**Paradise** Paradise a nickname for Celtic Park aka **Parkhead**

**Parkhead** the home ground of Celtic football club

**partan** crab

**paw** father

**pay-poke** pay packet

**pech** NORTH EAST struggle; puff
> **she came peching her way into...** she came puffing and panting into...
> **what a pech it was to get up that hill**

*a peel*

**peedie** In the Orkneys this means *little*.

**peel, peel tower** a Borders fortified tower

**peely-wally** pale and unhealthy looking

> the sunbed parlour lures the peely-wally
> the whole decor's a tad too peely-wally for my taste

**peenge** NORTH EAST OLDER SCOTS whinge

**peer** NORTH EAST poor

**peerie**[1] SHETLAND little

**peerie**[2] top, spinning top

**peever** SLANG hopscotch

**pend** arch; archway

**perr** poor

**photie** photo

**pibroch** a piece of music for the bagpipes consisting of a theme plus elaborate variations on the theme

**Picts** The first inhabitants of what was to become Scotland have left traces of their lives in the form of standing stones all over the country but particularly in the North East. Very little is known about these mysterious people, first referred to by a Roman writer in 297 AD, who seem to have disappeared by the middle of the 9th century, possibly overrun by the Scots, who moved across from the west.

**piece** also: 1) sandwich 2) slice of bread

**pinkie** the little finger (also used in northern parts of England and in the USA)

**pints** NORTH EAST [pronounced to rhyme with HINTS] shoelaces

**pish** SLANG piss

**pished** SLANG pissed, drunk

**pit¹** put

**pit²** IN PLACE NAMES It is thought that this is a Pictish word *pett* meaning *piece of land, place*. So **Pittenweem**: place of the cave; **Pitlochry**: place with the stones.

**Pittodrie** Aberdeen's football stadium

**plank** NORTH EAST hide; hide away

**plantie-crub** SHETLAND small round stone enclosure for growing cabbages

**plat** In the language of builders and architects this is a platform or a flat piece of stone or cement.

**play** If a person is said to be **playing himself/herself** this simply means that he/she is playing or having fun or playing around.

**playpiece** This is a snack for a schoolkid to eat at playtime, usually a biscuit or packet of crisps.

**pled** This is the standard Scots past simple of the verb *to plead*.

**plenishin** OLDER SCOTS furniture

**plook** zit, pimple

**plooky** covered with pimples

> **plooky or no, ah'm gonna snog him**

**plouk** same as **plook**

**plowter about** splash about, flounder about (*in water, in snow*)

**poind** LEGAL SCOTS [pronounced PIND to rhyme with SINNED] seize or impound (*goods for the payment of debt*)

**poinding** LEGAL SCOTS [pronounced PINDING] the seizure of goods for the payment of debt

**poke** (little) bag
**a poke of chips** a bag of chips

> **wi aw his worldly goods in an auld plastic poke**

**pokey hat** ice-cream cone

**policies** LEGAL SCOTS The **policies** of a property are the grounds round about it.

**polis** [the stress is reversed to give the pronunciation POH-lis] 1) police 2) policeman

**pooch** NORTH EAST pocket

**postie** postman; postwoman

**pouffe** In Scotland this piece of furniture is pronounced [pooFAY] not [poof]. Wonder why.

**pree** NORTH EAST OLDER SCOTS taste, sample

**press** a shallow cupboard set into a wall

**Prestonpans (Battle of)** This battle in September 1745 just to the east of Edinburgh saw the **Jacobites** under Bonnie Prince Charlie defeat the Hanoverian forces led by Sir John Cope. The result was significant not only because it constituted a psychological boost to the Jacobite cause but also because it meant that a large proportion of Scotland was now under Jacobite control.

**Prince Charlie (jacket)** the short jacket worn with the kilt

**principal teacher** head of department

**procurator fiscal** LEGAL SCOTS public prosecutor

**provost** mayor

**puckle** → **a puckle** a little; a few; several

**puddock** frog

**puff** → SLANG **in my puff** in my life
**on yer puff** on your own

**puirtith** NORTH EAST OLDER SCOTS poverty

**pure** GLASGOW

A common, especially Glaswegian, slang intensifier.
**ah pure wish ah could** I really wish I could
**pure dead brilliant** absolutely, totally brilliant
**his oxters were pure mingin** his armpits stank like nobody's business

**pursuer** LEGAL SCOTS plaintiff

**pus** SLANG face

# Qq

**quaich** a shallow, two-handled drinking vessel

**quean, quine, quinie** NORTH EAST girl

*a quaich*

# Rr

**ra**

> In Glaswegian speech the word *the* often turns into **ra** and merges with surrounding words.
> **werra keys?** where are the keys?
> **ye gonna gerra bus?** are you going to get the bus?
> **gorra cash?** got the cash?

**radge** EAST COAST SLANG crazy bastard; bastard
Also an adjective and adverb: crazy, wild
**seen the radge paintings the guy does?**
**going radge on the terraces** going wild on the terraces

**raffle** → **away ye go and raffle yourself** get knotted, get lost, don't bother me

**raivelt** NORTH EAST OLDER SCOTS confused

**rammy** fight, brawl

**randan** → **to go out on the randan** to go out to have a good time, round the pubs, clubs etc

**rare** This can also mean *great* or *brilliant*.
**and a right rare time was had by all** and we all had a great old time

**rasp** raspberry

**rax** NORTH EAST reach

**redd up** SHETLAND tidy

**reef** NORTH EAST roof

**reek** smoke

**reestit mutton** SHETLAND smoke-dried mutton

**reiver** raider, robber in the Scottish Borders in former times

**rerr** rare; great, tremendous

**reset** LEGAL SCOTS receive and sell on (*stolen goods*), fence (*stolen goods*); also used as a noun

> **McHarg was also sentenced to six months for reset**

**rhone** 1) gutter (*on the roof*) 2) short for **rhonepipe**

**rhonepipe** drainpipe

**rickle** → **she was just a rickle of banes** she was just a bag of bones, she was all skin and bones
**a rickle of stones** a heap of stones

**right** → **that'll be right!** a sarcastic way of disagreeing or saying *no, I don't think so*

> **me lend you £55? aye, that'll be right**

**rikkin lum** NORTH EAST a smoking chimney, therefore an inhabited house

**rin** NORTH EAST run

**rocklum** a chimney in a rockface

**Rockness** Loch Ness near Inverness is the setting for this Scottish open-air rock festival.

**rone** same as **rhone**

**ronepipe** same as **rhonepipe**

**ros, ross** IN PLACE NAMES from both the **Brittonic** and the Gaelic for promontory or wood. So **Kinross**: head of the cape.

**roup** LEGAL SCOTS auction

**rousht** NORTH EAST rust
**stick wi me n yer tackits'll niver rousht** I'll look after you (literally: stick with me and your hobnailed boots will never rust)

**row** [pronounced to rhyme with HOW]→ **to give somebody a row** to tell somebody off, to bawl somebody out

**rowth** NORTH EAST OLDER SCOTS a large number; a large amount **a fair rowth o money** quite a lot of money

**Royal Highland Show** One of the UK's largest agricultural shows, held in June every year just outside Edinburgh. Highlights include displays of animals, food and drink exhibitions and competitions.

**Royal Mile** The street leading from Edinburgh Castle down to Holyrood Palace. Going down from the castle, it's made up of Castlehill, Lawnmarket, High Street, Canongate and Abbey Strand.

*John Knox's house on the Royal Mile*

# Ss

**S1, S2** etc the first and second year etc in a secondary school

**saa** SHETLAND 1) saw 2) so

**sae** so

**saft** soft

**sair** 1) sore, painful 2) hard, difficult
A North East Scots idiom: **it's a sair fecht** it's a struggle

**sair erse** NORTH EAST SLANG moaner

**sannie** 1) sandwich 2) sandals, sandshoes

**sark** OLDER SCOTS shirt

**sarking** the boards or felt directly beneath the slates or tiles of a roof

**sasine** LEGAL SCOTS To give **sasine** to someone is to transfer legal ownership of feudal property to that person.

**Sasines** → LEGAL SCOTS **Register of Sasines** the land registry that records details of property ownership

**Sassenach** 1) Englishman; Englishwoman 2) English

**sauchie** from the Lowland Scots for *a place full of willows*. So **Sauchiehall Street**, Glasgow (**Sauchie Haugh**: low-lying ground covered with willow trees)

**-say** IN PLACE NAMES a common ending; but the actual derivation is the Norse word *ey* meaning island. So **Whalsay**: whale island.

**scaffie** NORTH EAST binman

**scants** pants, underpants

**scarf** SHETLAND shag (*the feathered type*)

**scart** NORTH EAST scratch

**scattald** SHETLAND common grazing land

**schemie** EAST COAST a person who lives on a housing estate or scheme, often referring to the adolescent hooligan or chav type (known as **neds** in the west). Also an adjective: **schemie life**

**schochle** NORTH EAST shuffle

**sclater** NORTH EAST slater (who works on roofs)

**sclim** OLDER SCOTS to climb

**scoobied** SLANG clueless, useless

**scooby** → **he diznae have a scooby** SLANG he doesn't have a clue (from rhyming slang, **scooby doo** = clue)

**scoocher** NORTH EAST beggar

**scoosh** SLANG do easily
**ah'll scoosh it** it'll be a doddle
**ah scooshed the exam** the exam was dead easy

**scoosh case** → SLANG
**the exam was a scoosh case** the exam was dead easy

**scorrie** seagull

**Scotch pie** go to the **Menu Reader**, page 145

## Scots, Scottish, Scotch

As an adjective **Scots** is normally used in connection with things linguistic, so you might talk about
  **a Scots word**
or
  **an old Scots usage**.
The Scots themselves find it irksome if someone says
  **he is Scots**.
It is preferable to say
  **he is Scottish**
or
  **he is a Scot**.                                              →

> The most generally used adjective is **Scottish**. You can't really go wrong with this one.
>
> The word **Scotch** is likely, if misused, to put backs up in Scotland. Basically **Scotch** is restricted to a smallish number of set collocations, for example
>
> > **Scotch broth, Scotch egg, Scotch mist, Scotch pie, Scotch whisky.**
>
> Never say of someone that
>
> > **he/she is Scotch!**

**scour about** NORTH EAST look around

**scran** SLANG food

**scratcher** SLANG bed
**ah'll bide in ma scratcher till lunchtime** I'm going to stay in bed until lunchtime

**scregh** screech, scream

> **the scregh of the wind**

**screive** OLDER SCOTS scribble

**scunner** disgust, put off
**I've scunnert masel wi...** I've had so much... that I'm sick of it
**would that no scunner ye!** that really is the limit!

> The word is also used as a noun.
> > **there's the old scunner** there's the old so-and-so
> > **the scunners!** the sods!

**scunnering** disgusting; irritating

**scunnert** disgusted; pissed off; fed up

**scutter aboot** NORTH EAST 1) mess about 2) chase about
Also used as a noun.
**getting everything ready for the party was a fair scutter aboot** it was some hassle getting everything ready

**sea-loch** a loch that is open to the sea

**see**

> 1) The word **see** can be used to point up the subject of a sentence, to make sure the listener realizes just who you are talking about before you say what you want to say about that person (which might well be yourself).
>   **see ma wife, she's no too pleased aboot this**
>   **she hates it, but see me, ah love it**
>   **see tapas, magic** tapas are absolutely fantastic.
>
> Note the amazing concision of the Scots here.
>
> 2) **See** in Scots can also be used to mean *to give.*
>   **see's a go on yer bike** give us a go on your bike
>   **see's back ma jaikit** give me my jacket back

**seek** → **he's never had his worries to seek** he has always had quite enough worries

**selkie** SHETLAND seal

> **Selkie** can also mean a mythical creature which sometimes takes the form of a seal and sometimes a person.

**Selkirk Grace** The Selkirk Grace is a fine and sonorous grace recited on **Burns Night**.

> Some hae meat and canna eat
> > And some wad eat that want it
> But we hae meat and we can eat
> > And sae let the Lord be thankit

> > *wad = would*
> > *want it = don't have it*
> > *sae = so*

**selt** sold

**sen** since

**sgian-dubh** [pronounced SKI-UN DOO]. This is the correct Gaelic spelling of **skean dhu**.

**shalder** SHETLAND oyster catcher

**shan** bad, disgraceful, shabby

**sharn** NORTH EAST OLDER SCOTS dung

**sheltie** a Shetland pony

**sheriff** LEGAL SCOTS equivalent to a JP in England

**Sheriff Court** LEGAL SCOTS Most Scottish towns will have a **Sheriff Court**, where a wide range of criminal and civil cases are heard. The High Court is reserved for trials of the most serious criminal offences.

**Sheriff officer** LEGAL SCOTS His duties include raising legal actions on instruction by a lawyer, collecting debts and delivering summonses.

**sherrikin** telling off

**shiel(in)** OLDER SCOTS shelter; hut

*shelties by the broch of Mousa*

**shilpet** SHETLAND sour

**shilpit** skinny, starved-looking

**shining bright** → RHYMING SLANG **that'll be shining bright** a humorous version of the ironic **that'll be right**, ie no, not likely, who do you think you're kidding

> **£120 for a pair a they jeans, aye that'll be shining bright**

> **shinty** Shinty is a fast-moving game played by two teams of 14 players each on a pitch that can be up to 145 metres by 90 metres. Both sides of the stick, known as a **caman** or **hurley**, can be used to strike →

shinty

the ball. The ball can be hit above head height (unlike in hockey). And swinging the stick above head height is also allowed.

**shoatie** → **to keep shoatie** to keep lookout

**shoogle** shake, wobble

hey, dinna shoogle they cans aboot

**shoogly** shaky, wobbly

**shoon** OLDER SCOTS shoes

**shop** → NORTH EAST **Dad's through the shop**

> In Aberdeen and the North East this means that *Dad is around the house somewhere* or that *Dad's in the next room* or that *Dad's in the next office.*

**short leet** shortlist

**shottie** → **to keep shottie** to keep lookout

**show of presents** a party held by a bride-to-be shortly before her wedding to show her friends the wedding presents she has been given

**shtumer** SLANG idiot

**shuggle** shake

**shuggly** shaky, wobbly

**shunky** SLANG toilet

**sic** such

**sicht** sight

**sick line** sick note, a note from a doctor confirming that a person is not fit for work

**sidieways** sideways

**siller** NORTH EAST OLDER SCOTS money

**simmer dim** SHETLAND the light night around mid-summer

**simmet** NORTH EAST vest; shirt

**single end** a tenement flat with just one room; no toilet; not many left these days

**single fish** a piece of fish without the chips, when buying a **fish supper**

**single malt** a malt whisky that is distilled with the grain and water of one particular area only, as opposed to a **blended**

**sitooterie** a humorous invented word for a conservatory (the sort that people have built onto the back of their houses to maximize the enjoyment of sunshine, or grow plants in)

**skaith** NORTH EAST wound

**Skara Brae** A storm in Orkney in 1850 uncovered the best preserved prehistoric village in northern Europe. Various houses are clearly visible along with connecting passageways, stone furniture and artefacts.

**skean dhu** an anglicised spelling variant of the Gaelic **sgian-dubh** [pronounced SKI-UN DOO]. This is the traditional dagger (though the standard modern Highland dress version can barely open an envelope), carried stuffed down the side of a sock, when the kilt is worn.

**skeelie, skeely** NORTH EAST OLDER SCOTS skilled

**skelf** splinter

**skelly-eyed** boss-eyed

**skelp** smack, hit
**ye're no allowed tae skelp yer wean these days** you're not allowed to smack your child these days

**skelpin** smacking, smack

**skime** gleam

**skink** go to the **Menu Reader**

**skirlie** NORTH EAST go to the **Menu Reader**

**skite** to slide; to slip
SLANG **oot onra skite** out getting boozed up

**skitie** slippery

**skitter** NORTH EAST 1) fiddly, time-consuming job 2) a very small amount
**ah've nae a skitter tae ma name** I've not a penny to my name

**skitters** → **the skitters** the runs, diarrhoea

**skoosh** 1) squirt 2) same as **scoosh**

**skoosher** a non-technical word for the windscreen washer on a car

**skreich of day** daybreak

**slàinte** a Gaelic word [pronounced SLAANJ] meaning *cheers!, your health!*; if you want to use a fuller variant, try saying: **slàinte mhath** [pronounced SLAANJUH VAH]. It means *good health*. Or **slàinte mhòr** [pronounced SLAANJUH VOR] which means literally *big health*.

**slaister** NORTH EAST 1) spill, dribble
2) a person who eats in a messy manner

**slater** woodlouse

**sleekit** sly, cunning

**sleep in** oversleep

> **sorry I'm late boss, I slept in**
> In Scotland this is a possible excuse (unlike in England where it would be the equivalent of saying **sorry I'm late boss, I decided to have a lie-in.**)

**slevvery** wet, slimy

**smeik** smoke

**smirr** drizzle
   **a smirr of snow** a light brushing of snow

**smorrin** NORTH EAST stuffed up
   **smorrin with the cold** stuffed up with a cold

**snaw bree** NORTH EAST OLDER SCOTS slush (*snow*)

**sneckit** snarled up, caught

**snib** door catch
   **to leave the door on the snib** to leave the door unlocked but shut with a catch so that it cannot be opened from the outside

**so**

> In combination with a verb this can be used as a way of emphasizing what has been said.
>    **he's right wee bastard, so he is**

**soapdodger** SLANG a dirty, smelly individual

**soapy bubble** GLASGOW RHYMING SLANG trouble

> **couldnae keep ootay the soapy bubble**

**solan** SHETLAND gannet

**some** → NORTH EAST **it was some much for them** it was too much for them

**sonsy** OLDER SCOTS beautiful, attractive in a plump and cheery sort of way

**sook** SLANG same as **souk**

**soor** sour

**sotter** NORTH EAST mess
**fit a sotter!** what a mess!

**souk** SLANG [pronounced SOOK] person who sucks up to people in authority

**spaegie** SHETLAND muscle ache after exertion

**spaiver** flies (*on trousers*)

**speir** [pronounced SPEAR] ask, enquire

**speuggie** sparrow

**spite** → **to have a spite against** to have it in for

**split-new** brand-new

**spoot** SHETLAND razor clam

**sporran** the large pouch, traditionally made of fur, that hangs from a man's belt in front of the kilt

**spud** NORTH EAST In the North East of Scotland if you have a **spud** in your tights, then you'll have a hole in them and not a potato.

**spuds** GLASGOW SLANG feet

**spunk** NORTH EAST a match (the kind you strike). But in the North East you wouldn't say *strike* – instead you **crack** a spunk.

**spurtle** a traditional porridge stirrer

**square go** a fight one to one

**Squinty Bridge** a new bridge over the Clyde in Glasgow, which crosses the river at an angle

**St Andrew's Day** Scotland's patron saint is celebrated every year on 30 November with various events throughout the country.

**St Kilda** St Kilda is an archipelago off the west coast of Scotland, beyond the Outer Hebrides. The islands have been uninhabited since 1930 when the remaining population requested evacuation back to the mainland because of the extreme isolation. The islands are now a World Heritage Site and comprise Europe's most important seabird colony.

**stance** In Scotland taxis wait at a **stance** not a *rank*. In times gone by a **stance** was an overnight stopping place for cattle on the move.

**Standard Grade** exams taken in Scotland at the end of the fourth year of secondary education

**stane** stone

**stank** drain; gutter

**stapped** → **the fridge is stapped** the fridge is stuffed full

**stappit full** stuffed full, crammed

**stave** sprain

> **he staved his ankle/finger**

**stay**

> In Scots **to stay** also means *to live.* This can be a source of some confusion for English people for whom the word **stay** has the connotation of something temporary. The following totally ridiculous conversation took place with a Glasgow taxi-driver.

> taxi-driver: **been staying in Glasgow long?**
> English passenger: **no, I live here**

**steamboats** SLANG drunk

> **steamie** A public washhouse, for washing clothes.
> They no longer exist but are a part of modern Scottish
> history, featuring in plays and novels.

**steamin** SLANG drunk

**steekit mist** SHETLAND thick fog

**stew** NORTH EAST In the North East **stew** is also *dirt*.

**stirk** bullock

**stoat** SLANG hit
**to stoat the baw** to knock a ball about

> But this also has an extended meaning: to be a
> pedophile; to be a child molester

**stoat-the-baw** SLANG child abuse; cradle snatching

**stoat down** SLANG pour down

**stoater** SLANG 1) an especially attractive girl 2) something
that is a very good example of its kind

> **yer mither wuz a wee stoater those days**
> **wan stoater of a dent you've got in your new motor**
> **there, eh?**

**stock jacket** the short jacket worn with the kilt

> **Stone of Destiny** Also known as the **Stone**
> **of Scone**, this stone has been used as part of
> enthronement ceremonies since the 9th century for
> Scottish, English and British monarchs. In 1296
> Edward I of England removed the stone from Scone, →

where it had been kept since Scone became the capital of the Scottish kingdom in around 840 AD, and took it to Westminster Abbey. There it remained (except for a brief period of 4 months in 1950 when it was repossessed by Scottish nationalists and left outside Arbroath Abbey) until its symbolic return to Scotland on **St Andrew's Day** 1996. It can now be seen alongside the **Honours of Scotland** in the Crown Room of Edinburgh Castle.

**Stone of Scone** same as **Stone of Destiny**

**Stonehaven fireball festival** Annual fire festival to welcome the New Year when locals swing large balls of burning material on the end of a wire in a procession through the town's streets.

**stookie** a plaster cast on a broken arm or leg

> Also used as a slang verb meaning *to hit* (Scots has an amazing number of verbs for this action).
> **he stookied him and ran off with his mobile**

**stoon** a small sharp pain

**stoor** 1) dust 2) a cloud of dust/smoke/steam etc

> In the North East if you burn something while cooking then a person coming into the room might say:
> **fit a stoor!**

**stooshie** same as **stushie**

**stot** bounce

> **the rain was fair stottin off the tent roof**

**stotious** SLANG drunk

**stoup** OLDER SCOTS jug, pitcher

*a strath*

**stour** same as **stoor**

**stovies** NORTH EAST go to the **Menu Reader**, page 143

**stowed out** packed, crowded

> the bar was stowed out, nae chance of a seat

**stramash** [pronounced with the stress on the last syllable] commotion; pushing and shoving

> a right stramash in the goalmouth there was until the ball was finally booted clear

**strath** from the Gaelic *srath* meaning *broad river plain*. So **Strathspey**: plain of the Spey; **Strathclyde**: plain of the Clyde.

**strippit** NORTH EAST OLDER SCOTS striped

**stushie** commotion, fuss, quarrel; fight

**suit**

> A Scot is more likely to say **you suit blue** than *blue suits you*.

**supper**

> If you go to a fish and chip shop you can have a **fish supper**, a **steak pie supper**, a **sausage supper** – these are served all day (not just at supper time) and will be chips plus fish/steak pie/sausage etc.

**swaabie** SHETLAND black-backed gull

**swadgie** SLANG look
   **gieza swadgie o yer mobile** give us a look at your mobile

**swallie** a drink
   **ah had a swallie wi Murdo efter** I had a couple of drinks with Murdo afterwards
   **a nice wee swallie** a nice drink

**swedge** SLANG fight

**swedgin** SLANG fighting

**sweetie wife** an effeminate sort of man, especially an older one

**swick** NORTH EAST cheat
   **to swick the queue** to jump the queue

**swither** be undecided; dither, hesitate

> I'm swithering between going out or staying in

**sybie, sybo** spring onion

**syne** OLDER SCOTS since; then; ago

# Tt

**T in the Park** annual pop music festival held over a weekend in July near Kinross, Fife

**tabbie** NORTH EAST cigarette end, dog-end

**tablet** type of sweet, like fudge but usually harder

**tacketties** big boots

**tackits** NORTH EAST big boots

**tae** to; too

**tail** → **with the ticket in ma tail** with the ticket in my pocket

**tak** take

**tammy** short for **Tam o'Shanter**, a man's round flat hat, no brim, with a bobble on top

**tammy norie** SHETLAND puffin

**tang** NORTH EAST seaweed

**Tannadice** the home stadium of Dundee United FC

**tap** 1) top 2) loan
    **he's always looking for a tap** he's always trying to
    borrow some money

**tappit** tufted (*of a chicken*)

**tapsalteerie** OLDER SCOTS topsy-turvy

**tattie-bogie, tattie bogle** NORTH EAST scarecrow

**tattie howkin** NORTH EAST potato harvesting

**tatties** 1) potatoes 2) NORTH EAST SLANG finished, done for;
    dead; in big trouble; rubbish
    **that report is tatties** that report is rubbish

    **tatties ower the side** done for, beat

**tawse** a leather strap as used by teachers for punishing
    schoolchildren, a practice which has now been abolished

**tay** IN PLACE NAMES from the Gaelic *taigh* meaning *house*. So
    **Taynuilt**: house on the stream.

**tea**

> In Scotland your **tea** is your supper, your main evening
> meal. The meal has generated some idioms.
>     **your tea's oot** you're in trouble
>     **I knew if I did that ma tea was oot** I knew if I did
>     that I would be in trouble
>     **your tea'll be up in a minute** you're heading for
>     trouble
>     **you'll have had your tea** Said to a visitor who drops
>     in just around supper time by someone who doesn't
>     really relish the idea of making a meal for this visitor,
>     since that would be too much effort or even involve
>     some expense. These days the expression is normally
>     used in a tongue-in-cheek way.

**tear** → NORTH EAST **to give someone a tear of lip** to be very cheeky or rude to someone

**teckit** SHETLAND thatched

**teen** took

**teip** NORTH EAST SLANG [pronounced TYPE] condom

**teip up** NORTH EAST SLANG wear a condom; put on a condom

**telt** told
**telt ye!** told you so!

**tenement** block of flats built on several storeys around a single entrance passage, known as a **close**; in Scotland the word tenement is not a pejorative term

*tenements*

**teuch** NORTH EAST tough, as in describing a piece of meat

**teuchter** [pronounced CHUCHTER] Highlander, though this has a slightly mocking overtone, so best not to call a Highlander a **teuchter** to his face (or to his friend's face).

**thae** those

**that**

> Some typically Scots constructions, puzzling to the non-Scot:
>
> **is that you had your lunch?** have you had your lunch?
> **is that you?** have you finished?; are you ready?; is that all you want?
> **that's me lost** I'm lost
> **is that them no finished yet?** aren't they finished yet?
> **that's the train just away** the train has just left
> **you tell him that and that'll be you** you'll be in trouble
>
> Here's a bit of chat when collecting dry-cleaning:
> **have ye got the ticket?**
> (shop assistant takes ticket): **that's us then** = right, thanks
>
> (shop assistant hands over dry-cleaning):
> **and that's you then** = there you are

**thegither** together

**they** those

> This is often assumed by English-speakers to be an incorrect usage. The word, also written **thae**, is in fact an old Scots plural form of *that*, quite distinct in origin (but not in sound) from the personal pronoun *they*.
> **he's got wanny they DVD players**
> he's got one of those DVD players

**thocht** NORTH EAST thought

**thole** tolerate, stand; endure

**thon** NORTH EAST that (over there); those (over there). North Eastern Scots has an extra word for *that* and *those* when the reference is more remote from the speaker.

**thought** → **it's a thought having to go back to work the next day** it's a daunting prospect...

**thrang** hectic

**thrapple** throat

**thrawn** awkward; argumentative; pig-headed

**through** → **to come through** can, in Central Scotland, mean either to come to Edinburgh from Glasgow or to come to Glasgow from Edinburgh
**is the kettle through the boil?** has the kettle boiled?

**throughby** OLDER SCOTS in the next room; into the next room

**throwe't** → NORTH EAST **to faa doon throwe't** to lapse unintentionally into the vernacular. This is said of someone who is attempting to speak posh and then gets it **wrang**.

**thunder-plump** thundery shower

**tig** → **to play tig** to play tag

**tigh** IN PLACE NAMES from the Gaelic *taigh* meaning *house*. So **Tighnabruaich**: house on the hill.

**tilly** IN PLACE NAMES from the Gaelic *tullach* meaning *hillock*. So **Tillicoultry**: (possibly) back land hill.

**Tim** SLANG derogatory for Catholic

**tim** empty

**tim oot** empty out

**timeous** LEGAL SCOTS In formal, official or legalistic Scots
**timeous** means *done in or at the proper time.*

> **... which duties and obligations shall be executed in
> a diligent and timeous manner**

**tink** 1) rascal; mischievous child
2) NORTH EAST a dirty individual, a social outcast

**tint** OLDER SCOTS lost

**tirrick** SHETLAND arctic tern

**tober** IN PLACE NAMES from the Gaelic *tobar* meaning *well.*
So **Tobermory**: Mary's well.

**toffee** NORTH EAST OLDER SCOTS In the North East
**toffee** can be what elsewhere in Scotland is called
**tablet**.

**toon** town

**toonser** NORTH EAST a townie; as opposed to a **teuchter**,
who comes from the country

**toorie** SHETLAND knitted hat

**tor** IN PLACE NAMES from the Gaelic *tòrr* meaning *hill.* So
**Kintore**: hill head.

**torn-faced** miserable looking

**totty** potato

**toty wee** tiny little

**tousie, towsie** 1) tangled
**the wee lassie's hair's all towsie**
2) rough and with a fair bit of foul play
**it's 15:0 to Hawks but a towsie game so far**

**trachle** NORTH EAST trudge; slog

**trachled** NORTH EAST harassed

**Trades** A traditional two-week industrial holiday in Aberdeen and Edinburgh, similar to the **Fair** in Glasgow.

**trang** SHETLAND busy; working well

**trauchle** NORTH EAST same as **trachle**

**Treaty of Union** This treaty, which came into force in May 1707, united Scotland and England under one parliament. They were to remain thus linked until 1999 when the Scottish parliament was re-established. Scotland's legal system and church have always remained independent.

**trig** 1) tidy; smart 2) alert

**trip** → **her face was tripping her** she was looking as miserable as sin, she had a face as long as a month of Sundays

**tron** In old Scottish towns goods and farm produce were weighed in a building called a **tron**, which housed the official public weighing scales. The Trongate is a major landmark in Glasgow.

**trow** SHETLAND similar to a *troll*

**trucking** barter

**tube** GLASGOW SLANG idiot

**tumshie** 1) turnip; swede 2) SLANG idiot

**tushkar** SHETLAND a spade used for cutting peat

**twa** OLDER SCOTS two

**twal** NORTH EAST twelve

**twa-three** NORTH EAST a couple (of), two or three

**ty** IN PLACE NAMES from the Gaelic *taigh* meaning *house*. So
  **Tyndrum**: house on the ridge.

**tyne** OLDER SCOTS lose

**tystie** SHETLAND black guillemot

# Uu

**uisge beatha** [pronounced **oosh**gih **beh**-uh] whisky; literally in the Gaelic: water of life

**unco** OLDER SCOTS very

**unco wheen** OLDER SCOTS a great number

**unnerstaun** understand

**Up-Helly-Aa** Annual Viking fire festival in Shetland where the life-size replica of a Viking ship is set on fire and launched out to sea.

## uplift

> This has an additional meaning in Scots, with nothing
> of the spiritual about it at all: it simply means to *collect*.
> **we'll get a van round to uplift your old sofa next
> Tuesday**

**upset price** another name, at an auction, for the reserve
price

**ur** are

**urnae** aren't

# Vv

**vennel** an old street, which as towns grew up, has shrunk to a lane or an alley

> **he owns a wee shop on Friars Vennel in Dumfries**

**voe** SHETLAND bay, creek (an old Norse word)

# Ww

**waa** NORTH EAST wall

**wabbit** knackered

**wallies** [pronounced to rhyme with SALLY'S] teeth

**wally close** tenement entrance and stairwell with tiled walls

**wally dug** (ornamental) china dog

**wame** NORTH EAST stomach, belly

**wan** [pronounced to rhyme with PAN] one

**wance** once

**wark** OLDER SCOTS work

**warrant sale** LEGAL SCOTS sale of some of a debtor's goods

**wasted** 1) drunk 2) exhausted 3) both of the former together

**water** → NORTH EAST **ower the water** in jail

**watter** → **doon the watter** down the Clyde on a pleasure steamer. Going **doon the watter** was a traditional Glasgow holiday; a boatload of families and couples and groups would sail down the Clyde to resorts such as Largs and Rothesay and the Kyles of Bute, traditionally (especially below decks) consuming vast quantities of alcohol.

**wattrie** NORTH EAST OLDER SCOTS toilet

**wauner** OLDER SCOTS wander

**wayleave** LEGAL SCOTS A right enabling land to be used by parties other than the owner, eg by the water authorities to lay pipes.

**wean** [pronounced WAYNE] child; more of a Glaswegian and West of Scotland word; elsewhere the usual word is **bairn**

**wecht** NORTH EAST weight

**wee** little

> **Wee Free** a member of the Free Church of Scotland; the term is, as it sounds, mocking and so obviously best not used to address such a church-goer directly. The Wee Frees are typically seen as the last bastion of good old traditional puritanism.

**wee half** a small whisky

**wee heavy** a very strong and sweetish beer, similar to barley wine

**Weedgie** Glaswegian, usually said by non-Glaswegians

**weel** SHETLAND NORTH EAST well

**well**

> Can be moved to the end of a sentence in Scots, to lend emphasis.
> **put yer jaikit on well**

**well on** nicely filled up with booze

**well seen** clear, obvious
**it's well seen you've done that before** it's obvious you've done that before

**well-fired** of a bread roll; very crisp, quite black on the outside

**well-kent** well-known

**went** → **I have went; he has went** etc This is a common Scottish use of the preterite in place of the past participle, especially in Glaswegian dialect. Some of those who use it in speech, would not use it in writing.

**wha, whae** who

**wheech** move quickly

**wheech away** whip away

**wheen** → **a fair wheen of them** quite a number of them

**wheesht** same as **whisht**

**whiles** NORTH EAST sometimes

**whin bush** gorse bush

**whin(s)** gorse

**whisht!** quiet!, hush!, sh!
   **haud yer whisht** be quiet, sh

**whisky mac** whisky with green ginger, amazing on a cold
   **dreich** day

**whit** what

**white settler** NORTH EAST If you've moved to the North East
   then you'll be a **white settler** not only if you come from
   England but if you come from any other part of Scotland
   too.

**whitrat** NORTH EAST OLDER SCOTS weasel

**whulp** puppy

**whyles** NORTH EAST sometimes

**wi** with

**wide** SLANG cheeky, out of order
   **they were pure getting wide** they were pushing their luck

**wide-o** SLANG crook, conman, villain

   **this travel company's a bunch a wide-os, ah want
   ma money back!**

**widna, widnae** wouldn't

**wifie** NORTH EAST woman

   **the wifie that runs the sweetie shop**

**wight** OLDER SCOTS strong

**wimplin** winding

**windae, windy** window
  **that's wur pay rise oot ra windae** that's our pay rise out
  the window

**wir** our

**wis** SHETLAND 1) was 2) us

**wish** → **do you wish another cup?** would you like
  another cup? This is not absurdly formal in Scots, as it
  would be in England.

**workie** workman

**wrang** wrong

> Here's an old Scottish joke. A man goes into a cake
> shop, points at a cake and asks:
>   is that an éclair or a meringue?
> The lassie answers:
>   no, no, you're right enough, it's an éclair

**writ** LEGAL SCOTS legal document; not like an English writ,
  which is a summons

**writer** LEGAL SCOTS In legal Scots a writer is a lawyer. It's not
  a spoken form.

**wur** our

**wursels** ourselves

**wye** NORTH EAST way

**wynd** 1) lane 2) stone staircase, usually to the basement
  level of a house

**wyte** NORTH EAST know

# Yy

**ya bass** you bastard; also appended to names by grafitti-writing gangs, really just as an indication of attitude to the world

**yacks** SLANG eyes

> there it was right under ma yacks

**yae** NORTH EAST one

**yaks** same as **yacks**

**yark** NORTH EAST yank, jerk

**ye** you

**yestreen** OLDER SCOTS last night; yesterday evening

**yett** OLDER SCOTS gate

**yin** one (*people or things*)

> have ye tried using a different yin?
> he's a strange yin, that Stanley

**yince** once

**yirded** NORTH EAST filthy

**yiz** rendering of **youse**

**yoal** SHETLAND a type of six-oared boat

**yon**

> Means both the singular *that... (over there)* and the plural *those... (over there)*; unlike the antiquated word *yonder* in English, this is still in use in Scots, mainly in the east.
>
> **gies yon pair a pliers and haud the ladder still**
> **what d'ye cry yon fella that's just become an MSP?**

**Yon** can also be used to refer to a person.
**he's nae match for big Shuggie, yon** he's no match for big Shuggie, that guy over there

**yon time** late; a long time

**it'll be yon time before we're hame**

**youse** GLASGOW

This is a plural form of *you* – an area in which Scots comes closer in structure to other European languages; though it is a dialect form, not used by all, and those who do use it in speech wouldn't normally write it. It's useful to be able to distinguish though and make it clear that you are talking about a group not an individual.
**youse played better today** you all (you, the team) played better today

**yowe** [pronounced to rhyme with COW] ewe

# Scottish
## Food and Drink

*A Menu Reader*

# Soups

**broth** thick, meal-in-a-plate type of soup, a staple item which varies according to the meat, fish, game or vegetables in season

**cock-a-leekie** traditional broth made with chicken, leeks, onions and rice

**Cullen skink** traditional broth (skink) of Finnan haddock, potatoes, onion and milk from the fishing village of Cullen

**ham and lentil broth** traditional broth made with a ham bone, lentils, carrot, turnip and parsley

**hotch potch** traditional broth made with lamb and fresh seasonal vegetables

**mussel broth** traditional soup made with mussels in their shells, onions and cooking liquor

**partan bree** crab (partan) broth (bree) made with vegetables, thickened with rice and cream

**Scotch broth** traditional soup made with boiling beef, whole pearl barley and dried peas, fresh vegetables in season (usually including turnips and carrots) finished with chopped parsley

# Main courses

## *Meat*

**Aberdeen Angus beef** from cattle specially bred on Scotland's rich pasturelands for prime quality flavour and succulence

**Arbroath smokie** copper-coloured, deheaded, whole haddock, mildly salted, hot smoked till cooked, eaten heated with butter

**blackface lamb** hardy Scots breed of small-sized sheep with fine flavoured meat

**bridie (Forfar)** beef steak and onion filling in 'lucky' horseshoe-shaped short pastry crust (originally for bride's wedding meal)

**brisket** beef cut, often rolled and salted for boiling with root vegetables

**buckie** whelk

**Forfar bridie** see bridie

**gigot** leg of lamb

**grouse** medium sized game bird (one per portion) with a darker flesh and stronger flavour than most other game birds; usually roasted

**guga (Solan goose)** salted young gannet, traditional to the Hebrides, eaten with floury potato and a glass of milk

**haggis supper** chippie's version, sausage-shaped, coated in batter, deep fried and eaten with chips

**haggis with neeps and tatties** haggis made from sheep's innards, oatmeal, onion and spices, boiled in the stomach bag, traditionally eaten with mashed swedes/turnips (neeps) and mashed potatoes (tatties)

**haunch of venison** hind leg of deer meat from a red deer or a roe deer, usually roasted and served with rowan jelly

**Highland beef** from a special breed of hardy cattle with thick hairy coats, grazed on Scotland's rich pasturelands to yield high-quality succulent meat

**hough (potted)** [pronounced HOCH, with och as in LOCH] cut of beef from lower end of the leg or shin, cooked till tender and set in jelly

**jugged hare** slow-cooked mature hare stew, usually served with floury potato

**Lorne sausage** *see* square sausage

**mealie pudding (white pudding)** savoury sausage, with oatmeal and onions, often shaped in loops or as slicing sausage

**mince and tatties** minced beef, stewed with onions and sometimes carrots and turnips, served with mashed potatoes (tatties)

**mutton** mature, over a year old, sheep

**pope's eye steak** prime cut of beef from the rump end, grilled or fried, known in England as rump steak

**reestit mutton** (*Shetland*) cuts of mature sheep, salted, dried and used for flavouring broths, best cuts kept for **Up-Helly-Aa** festivities in January

**rib eye steak** prime cut of beef from the back with an 'eye' of fat in the middle for succulence

**rumbledethumps** mashed potatoes, cooked cabbage and butter mixed together and served in a pie dish with grated cheese on top

**rump steak** cut of beef from the rump end which is usually stewed in Scotland, it is a less tender cut than an English rump steak

**sausage links** beef or pork meat minced with seasonings and a starchy filler, used to fill sausage skins, divided into links

**smokie (Arbroath)** *see* Arbroath smokie

**square sausage** fresh beef sausage made in a square shaped tin, cut in slices and known in Glasgow as a Lorne sausage

**stovies** sliced potatoes, onions and dripping (surplus fat from cooking beef, lamb, pork or bacon) slow-cooked in a pot, sometimes with chopped meat added

**white pudding** *see* mealie pudding

## Fish

**Finnan haddock** whole, split open haddock, lightly salted, delicately smoked, pale straw coloured, from the North East

**fish 'n' chips** deep-fried batter-coated fish (usually haddock) bought from the 'chippie' in Scotland, in the West eaten with salt and vinegar, in the East with salt and brown sauce

**fried herring in oatmeal** fresh filleted herring, pressed into oatmeal and shallow fried till brown on both sides, eaten with floury potatoes and butter

**kipper (Mallaig kipper, Loch Fyne kipper)** whole herring, split open, lightly salted and cold smoked, eaten at breakfast or teatime

**potted herring** filleted herring, rolled up and baked in vinegar and water with spices, served cold with salad

**salt herring** whole, gutted herring dry salted in barrels for several months, eaten with floury potatoes for 'tatties 'n' herrin'

**soused herring** same as potted herring

## Vegetables

**champit** or **chappit tatties** mashed potatoes

**clapshot** (*Orkney*) mashed potatoes and turnips/ swedes, beaten together and often served as vegetables with haggis

**floury (or mealy) potato** dry potato preferred in Scotland, popular varieties are Golden Wonder and Kerr's Pink

**kail** *or* **kale** traditional, hardy green winter vegetable of the cabbage family

**neeps** swedes, yellow turnips; traditional with haggis (neeps and tatties)

**nettle** green vegetable, tender young tops, eaten in springtime, often in a puréed soup

**sybo** spring onion

## Side dishes

**skirlie** oatmeal, onions and dripping (surplus fat from cooking beef, lamb, pork or bacon) fried in a pan and eaten with floury potatoes or roast or stewed meat

## Snacks

**bacon and egg roll** fried bacon and egg, served hot in a soft roll or bap for breakfast or snack

**gammon roll** soft roll filled with cooked ham, also known as gammon

**Scotch pie** small, hand-held, round, raised pie of cooked minced beef with top edge extending beyond the round of pastry covering the filling

**tablet** sweet confection made with butter, sugar and condensed milk, slightly harder in texture than fudge

# Cheese

**caboc** a very creamy Scots cheese, rolled in oatmeal; it may taste more like cream than cheese, since it contains no rennet

**crowdie** sharp, acidic, soft, cow's milk cheese either plain or with flavourings such as pepper and garlic

**Dunlop cheese** hard, pale yellow, cow's milk cheese from Ayrshire with a mellow, nutty flavour and creamy texture

# Drinks

**Atholl brose** medium oatmeal soaked in whisky, sieved and flavoured with heather honey, taken at New Year

**blended whisky** mix of pot still malt whisky (40%) and patent still grain whisky (60%) from different distilleries

**heather ale** amber gold, flowery aromatic cask beer with a bitter note, made from heather flowers and sold by its Gaelic name 'Fraoch'

**heavy** beer; closest thing to English bitter

**Irn Bru®** orange-gold, carbonated, non-alcoholic drink with a sweet-spicy flavour and a citrus tang, often described as Scotland's other national drink

**single and vatted malt whisky** distilled in a pot still from fermenting malted barley, 'single' is the product of one distillery only, 'vatted' comes from a number of different malt whisky producing distilleries

**whipkull** whipped egg yolks, sugar and rum: a Shetland drink taken at New Year breakfast with shortbread

**whisky mac** whisky with green ginger wine: a warming drink in cold weather

# Desserts

**apple frushie** open fruit tart, from an old Scots word for brittle or crumbly (referring to the pastry)

**blaeberry** like a bilberry

**bramble** black and juicy autumn berry, known in England as a blackberry

**burnt cream** rich cream custard with sugar crust 'burnt' on top to a hard crack

**clootie dumpling** large, celebration, spicy fruit pudding boiled in a cloth (clootie), served with custard or soft brown sugar (traditional for birthdays, Christmas and New Year); also sometimes fried with bacon and eggs for breakfast

**cranachan** harvest-home dish made by mixing cream and/or soft cream cheese with ripe soft berries, toasted oatmeal, heather honey and whisky

**Ecclefechan butter tart** open tart with a sweet buttery filling of dried fruit and walnuts

**grosset fool** gooseberry fool

## Ingredients

**Ayrshire bacon** salt-cured pig, back and streaky cuts rolled into a round, cut thinly and cooked till crisp

**heather honey** thick, strongly aromatic, full-flavoured honey, gathered by bees from ling or bell heather

**oatmeal** made from the oat grain which is ground into fine, medium and coarse grades, Scotland's staple grain

**rolled oats** flaky oats, made by steaming and rolling whole oats, used for a quickly made porridge

**whelk** shellfish from Scotland's shores; the Scots whelk is an English winkle

## Preserves

**rowan jelly** sweet preserve, made from whole rowan berries, served with venison and other game

# Baking

**Abernethy biscuit** less rich shortbread made for his patients by the 18th century Dr Abernethy

**bannock** large round plain scone or rich yeast bread, originally baked on a large round iron girdle

**bap** soft white bread roll, dusted with flour, sometimes square-shaped

**beremeal bannock** (*Orkney*) [pronounced BARE-meal] flat, round, girdle-baked, teatime bread made with ancient bere (barley) grown in Orkney and the North

**black bun** dense cake with dried fruits, highly spiced and enclosed in a pastry crust: a New Year speciality with whisky

**buttery rowie** (*Aberdeen*) misshapen, flaky, crisp roll (rowie), original to the North East, a croissant without the elegant shape

**cookie** rich yeast bun, eaten at teatime

**cream cookie** rich teatime yeasted bun, sliced open, filled with whipped cream and dusted on top with icing sugar

**crumpet** thinner and larger than the Scots pancake, girdle-baked, smooth on one side and lacy on the other, eaten rolled up with butter and/or jam for afternoon tea

**currant loaf** light, sweet, yeasted bread, traditionally eaten at teatime, sometimes toasted with butter

**dropped scones** alternative name for Scotch pancakes, 'dropped' onto the girdle

**Dundee cake** fruit cake with sultanas, orange peel and whole almonds on top, originally a by-product of marmalade making in Dundee

**gingerbread** spicy fruit loaf made with treacle and ginger, eaten at teatime

**girdle scone** any kind of sweet or savoury scone baked on a heated flat iron plate, known as a girdle

**oatcake** thin, crisp, savoury biscuit made with oatmeal: originally baked on the girdle and eaten with butter and cheese as a staple item of diet

**pancake (Scotch)** sweet, golden brown, flat round disc, made with the same batter mixture as Scotch crumpet: eaten with butter and jam at teatime (an American pancake is its larger version); not like crêpe

**petticoat tails** shortbread round, cut in wedges but with a small circle cut out of the centre, resembling the crinoline petticoat

**potato scone** same as tattie scone

**rowie** *see* **buttery rowie**

**Selkirk bannock** rich, buttery, round, curved on top, yeasted bread with sultanas: sliced and toasted with butter for tea

**shortbread** butter, sugar and flour, blended and

shaped into rounds, fingers or triangles, baked
slowly till pale golden and crisp

**soda scone** round plain scone, baked on a girdle,
eaten with butter and jam for tea

**softie** round, yeasted, slightly sweet, soft morning
roll from the North East, (as distinct from the harder
buttery rowie)

**square loaf** straight-sided loaf with close-textured
soft crumb sides, slices cut in half used to sandwich
the Lorne/square sausage

**tattie scone** thin, unleavened triangular-shaped
scone, made with a mixture of mashed potatoes and
flour, baked on both sides till brown on a girdle

## sundries

**black pudding** blood sausage, flavoured with
spices, oatmeal and onion, usually shaped in loops
or as slicing sausage; accompanies a traditional
breakfast

**brose** dish made from oatmeal and water or milk

**porridge** fine, medium or coarse oatmeal boiled
in water till thick, seasoned with salt and eaten for
breakfast with milk or cream

*Here's a smattering of* **Gaelic.**

## good morning
madainn mhath
[madeen **va**]

## hello (*during the day*)
latha math
[laa **ma**]

> Buy a Gael a dram and ask him/her to tell you how to say 'I' here!

## good evening
feasgar math
[fesgar **ma**]

## good night
oidhche mhath
[uh-ee-*kh*ih **va**]

> the *kh* as in Ba*ch*, lo*ch*

## goodbye
slàn leibh
[**slaan** luh-eev]

## thanks
tapadh leibh
[tah-puh **luh-eev**]

## thank you very much
mòran taing
[moh-ran **ta-eenk**]

## not for me
chan ann dhomhsa
[*kh*an a-oon gh**oh**suh]

> Buy a Gael a dram and ask him/her to tell you how to say 'gh'!

## please
mas e ur toil e
[mash uh oor **tol** uh]

*Gaelic*

**great!**
math dha-rìribh!
[ma gha **ree**riv]

**good**
math
[ma]

**that one**
am fear sin
[ihm **fair** shin]

**this one**
am fear seo
[ihm **fair** sho]

**not that one**
chan e am fear sin
[*kh*any**eh** ihm fair shin]

**I like it**
's toil leam e
[**stul** luhmuh]

**I don't like it**
cha toil leam e
[*kha* **tul** luhmuh]

**cheers!**
slàinte! *or* slàinte mhòr!
[sl**aa**njuh, slaanjuh **vor**]

**that was excellent**
bha sin sgoinneil
[va shin **skun**yel]

**I don't understand**
chan eil mi a' tuigsinn
[*kh*an yel mee uh **teek**shin]

There are no words given here for *yes* or *no*, because Gaelic is one of those languages that doesn't have a single way of saying *yes* or *no*. It all depends on what the question or statement is to which yes/no is the response.

Here are some Scottish **place names** which are not pronounced as you might think, as well as a few which may seem altogether unpronounceable.

The letters kh are pronounced like the ch in the way Scots say **loch**. Or like in the composer **Bach**.

| | |
|---|---|
| **Achiltibuie** | Akhil-tee-bOO-ee |
| **Alford** | AA-ford |
| **Altnabreac** | Altna-brake |
| **Avoch** | Awkh |
| **Ballachulish** | BallaHOOlish |
| **Balquhidder** | Balwidder |
| **Benbecula** | BenBECula |
| **Berwick** | Berrick |
| **Broughty Ferry** | Brotty Ferry |
| **Buccleuch** | Buh-KLOO |
| **Buchanan** | Byoo-KANan |
| **Cockburn** | COH-burn |
| **Colquhoun** | Co-HOON |
| **Crichton** | CRY-ton |
| **Culross** | CURE-oss |
| **Culzean** | Cuh-LAYN |
| **Dalry** | Dal-RYE |
| **Dalziel** | Dee-EL |
| **Drymen** | Drimmen |
| **Eigg** | Egg |

| | |
|---|---|
| **Findochty** | FinNE*kh*ty |
| **Fionnphort** | Finnerfort |
| **Footdee** | Fitty |
| **Friockheim** | Freekim |
| **Garioch** | Geery |
| **Glamis** | Glams |
| **Govan** | Guvn |
| **Grandtully** | Grantly |
| **Gullane** | Gullan *or* Gillan |
| **Hawick** | Hoyk |
| **Ingliston** | Ingleston |
| **Islay** | Isle-uh |
| **Keil** | Keel |
| **Kilconquhar** | KinYOO*kh*ar |
| **Kingussie** | Kin-YOO-see |
| **Kirkcaldy** | KirCODee |
| **Kirkcudbright** | KirCOObree |
| **Kyleakin** | Kile-Akin |
| **Langholm** | LANGam |
| **Lesmahagow** | Lezma-HAY-go |
| **Leuchars** | LOO-*kh*ers |
| **Linnhe, Loch** | Linny |
| **Mearns** | Mairns |
| **Milngavie** | Mul-GUY |
| **Moray** | Murray |

*Place names and whisky names*

| | |
|---|---|
| **Penicuik** | Penny-cook |
| **Sanquhar** | Sanker |
| **Sauchiehall Street** | So*khie*-hall *or* Sockie-hall Street |
| **Sciennes** | Sheens |
| **Scone** | Skoon |
| **Stranraer** | StranRAR |
| **Strathaven** | STRAYven |
| **Taynuilt** | TAYnult |
| **Tighnabruaich** | TinaBROO-a*kh* |
| **Tillicoultry** | TilliCOOtree |
| **Uig** | Oo-ig |
| **Urquhart** | URkurt |
| **Wemyss Bay** | Weems Bay |
| **Yetholm** | Yettam |

*From the huge range of* **whiskies** *produced in Scotland here is just a very small selection, chosen simply on the basis of their need for a pronunciation guide. In some cases you may hear more than one pronunciation used by the Scots themselves. There is not always a single correct pronunciation and a lot can depend on the strength of the Gaelic influence.*

| | |
|---|---|
| **Aberlour** | the our is as in 'our' or 'sour' |
| **Allt-a-Bhainne** | Alt-a-VAN-yuh, *though* Alt-a-VAYN *is heard too* |
| **An Cnoc** | An Noc *or if Gaelic* An Croc |

| | |
|---|---|
| **Auchentoshan** | O*khen*-toshan |
| **Bruichladdich** | Broo*kh*-LADdi*kh* |
| **Bunnahabhain** | Boona-HA-vin |
| **Caol Ila** | Cull EEla *or* Curl EEla |
| **Cardhu** | CarDOO |
| **Clynelish** | Cline-leesh |
| **Dailuaine** | Dal-YOO-an *or more Gaelic* Dal-OO-uhn-yuh |
| **Edradour** | the our is as in 'our' or 'sour' |
| **Glen Garioch** | Glen Geery |
| **Glen Glassaugh** | Glen Glasso*kh or* Glen Glassa |
| **Glen Mhor** | Glen Vor |
| **Glenmorangie** | the stress is on the 'mor' not on 'an', like saying the word 'orangey' |
| **Islay Mist** | Isle-uh Mist |
| **Laphroaig** | La-FROYG |
| **Ledaig** | Ledayg *or more Gaelic* Lejik |
| **Te Bheag** | Chay Vek (and no, not 'tea bag') |
| **Tomatin** | TomATin |
| **Tomintoul** | Tomin-TOWEL |

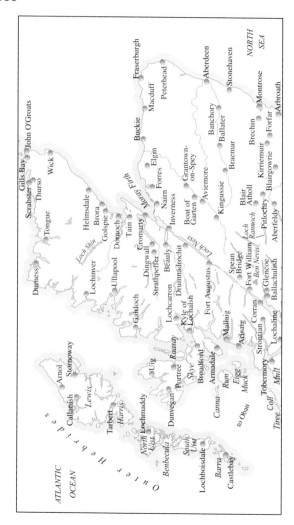

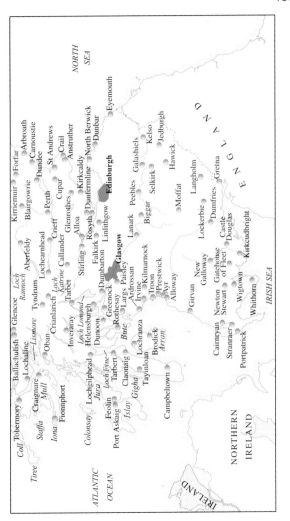

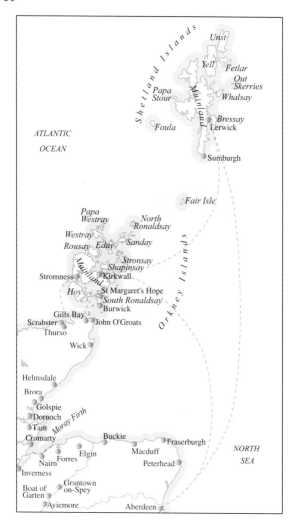

ATLANTIC
OCEAN

Shetland Islands

Unst

Yell

Fetlar

Out
Skerries

Whalsay

Papa
Stour

Mainland

Foula

Bressay
Lerwick

Sumburgh

Fair Isle

Papa
Westray

North
Ronaldsay

Westray

Rousay  Eday  Sanday

Mainland

Stronsay
Shapinsay

Stromness

Kirkwall

Hoy

St Margaret's Hope

South Ronaldsay

Gills Bay  Burwick

Scrabster
Thurso

John O'Groats

Orkney Islands

Wick

Helmsdale

Brora

Golspie

Dornoch

Tain

Cromarty

Moray Firth

Buckie

Fraserburgh

Elgin

Macduff

Forres

Nairn

Peterhead

Inverness

Boat of
Garten

Grantown
on-Spey

Aviemore

Aberdeen

NORTH
SEA